C000260065

•Barthol

Cycling
the
South Downs

Bartholomew
An imprint of HarperCollins*Publishers*

Published by Bartholomew
An imprint of HarperCollins*Publishers*
77-85 Fulham Palace Road
London W6 8JB

First published 1997
© Bartholomew 1997

Routes compiled by Peter McGrath,
except route 18, compiled by Ron Strutt
Designed by Creative Matters Design Consultancy, Glasgow

Photographs reproduced by kind permission of the following:
International Photobank pages 11, 34, 37, 38, 49, 73, 110;
Bill Meadows Picture Library pages 5, 15, 24, 26, 57, 69, 85;
The National Trust Photographic Library pages 8, 20, 87, 101, 105;
Tony Sullivan page 45; Maurice and Marion Teal page 50;
Andy Williams pages 29, 33, 41, 42, 61, 65.

Printed in Hong Kong

ISBN 0 7028 3511 0
97/1/16

CONTENTS

KEY TO ROUTES

Route			Grade	Distance km (miles)		Time to allow	Page
	1	Singleton Museum to Goodwood and the Trundle	moderate	15	(9.5)	1-3 hours	14
	2	The Cuckoo Trail – Polegate to Heathfield	easy	17.5	(11)	1-3 hours	17
	3	Alfriston Village and Drusillas Park Zoo	moderate	18.5	(11.5)	2 hours	19
	4	Selsey Bill – a short, flat tour by the sea	easy	22	(13.5)	2 hours	22
	5	Bentley Wildfowl and Motor Museum	moderate	25.5	(16)	2-4 hours	25
	6	Amberley to Shoreham on the South Downs Way	strenuous	25.5	(16)	3 hours	28
	7	Fishbourne to Chichester – a ride through history	easy	28.5	(17.5)	1-3 hours	32
	8	Battle of Hastings loop – a tour of 1066 country	moderate	29.5	(18.5)	2 hours	36
	9	Plaistow loop – Sussex wine and crafts	moderate	30.5	(19)	2-4 hours	40
	10	Ashdown Forest and the Bluebell Railway	moderate	32	(20)	2-3 hours	44
	11	Stedham Common to the foot of the Downs	moderate	33.5	(21)	2-3 hours	48
	12	Lewes to Eastbourne on the South Downs Way	strenuous	35.5	(22)	2-3 hours	52
	13	Bexley Hill and West Sussex villages	strenuous	39.5	(24.5)	2-4 hours	56
	14	Herstmonceux Castle via the Cuckoo Trail	moderate	43	(27)	2-4 hours	60
	15	Selborne's natural history and the Meon Valley	moderate	57	(35.5)	3-5 hours	64
	16	Petworth House and the north west Weald	strenuous	58	(36)	4 hours	68
	17	Pevensey Levels to Brightling and Battle	strenuous	59.5	(37)	3-5 hours	72
	18	Weald and Downs ride to Bramber Castle	strenuous	62.5	(39)	4-6 hours	76
	19	Hollycombe to Haslemere along the foot of the Downs	strenuous	63	(39)	3-5 hours	80
	20	Pevensey Bay to Bewl Bridge Reservoir	strenuous	65	(40.5)	4-6 hours	84
	21	Three castles loop – Pevensey, Bodiam and Herstmonceux	moderate	65	(40.5)	3-5 hours	88
	22	Top of the Downs to the Forest Ridge	strenuous	68.5	(42.5)	5 hours	92
	23	The South Downs Way – Petersfield to Bignor	strenuous	69	(43)	5-6 hours	96
	24	Bognor Regis, Selsey Bill and Chichester Harbour	moderate	93	(58)	5-7 hours	100
	25	The South Downs Way and the Downs Link	strenuous	112.5	(70)	8-12 hours	106

Distances have been rounded up or down to the nearest 0.5km (mile).

Route colour coding

undemanding rides compiled specifically with families in mind
15-25km (10-15 miles)

middle distance rides suitable for all cyclists
25-40km (15-25 miles)

half-day rides for the more experienced and adventurous cyclist
40-60km (25-40 miles)

challenging full-day rides
over 60km (over 40 miles)

grande randonnée – a grand cycling tour
100km (60 miles)

 Routes marked with this symbol are off-road or have off-road sections.

Windmill and St Mary's Church at Shipley (see Route 18)

LOCATION MAP

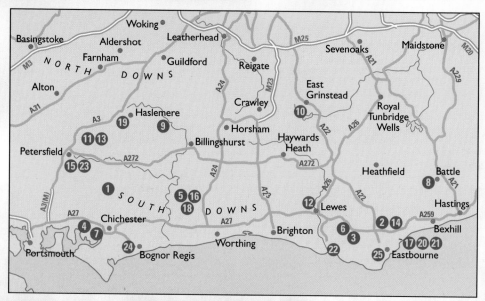

KEY TO ROUTE MAPS

M23	Motorway	Cycle route	P Parking
A259	'A' road / Dual carriageway	Optional route	☎ Telephone
B2130	'B' road / Dual carriageway	Start of cycle route	⊼ Picnic site
	Good minor road	12 Route direction	▲ Camping site
	Minor road	B Place of interest	🚻 Public toilets
	Track / bridleway	Public house	Viewpoint
	Railway / station	Café / refreshments	† Place of worship
	Canal / river	✗ Restaurant	Golf course
	Lake	Convenience store	Tumulus
50	Contour (height in metres)		
	Urban area	Height above sea level	
	Woodland		

Height above sea level

50	100	150	200 metres
165	330	490	655 feet

INTRODUCTION

How to use this guide

Bartholomew's *Cycling the South Downs* has been devised for all those who want trips out on their bicycles along quiet roads and tracks, passing interesting places and convenient refreshment stops without having to devise their own routes. Each of the 25 routes in this book has been compiled and ridden by an experienced cyclist for cyclists of all abilities.

Cycling the South Downs is easy to use. Routes range from undemanding rides compiled specifically with families in mind to challenging full-day rides; the type of route is easily identified by colour coding (see page 5). At the start of each route an information box summarises: total distance (in kilometres/miles – distances have been rounded up or down throughout to the nearest 0.5km/mile and are approximate only); grade (easy, moderate or strenuous based on distance and difficulty); terrain; an average time to allow for the route; directions to the start of the route by car and, if appropriate, by train.

Each route is fully mapped and has concise, easy-to-follow directions. Comprehensive information on places of interest and convenient refreshment stops along each route are also given. Accumulated mileages within each route description give an indication of progress, while the profile diagram is a graphic representation of gradients along the route. These should be used as a guide only.

The following abbreviations are used in the route directions:

LHF	left hand fork
RHF	right hand fork
SO	straight on
SP	signpost
TJ	T junction
TL	turn left
TR	turn right
XR	crossroads

Cycling the South Downs

The rides in this book cover some of the most beautiful and historic countryside that Britain has to offer. The rides run through the South Downs and the Weald that lies inland from the Downs, landscape that was first formed during the geological upheavals that formed the Alps. Both the South Downs and the Weald are hilly, and few of the routes in this book escape without hills in the ride.

The routes are intended to stay away from busy main roads as much as possible, and to allow cyclists to discover the peaceful back lanes and bridleways that cross the country, passing stately homes, castles and museums along the way. While suffering from being close to London and being crossed by many major roads, the back lanes have remarkably little traffic. Many of the villages have preserved their traditional character which can be seen in the village stores, country pubs and village greens you will see along these routes.

Geology, geography and history

The South Downs run from the Hampshire/West Sussex border to the Beachy Head cliffs in East Sussex. Their character is governed by the chalk rock that lies under the soil, which allows a range of otherwise rare alkaline-loving plants to flourish. The South Downs typically have a steep scarp slope that faces inland, and a more gentle dip slope that runs towards the coast, levelling into a coastal plain before meeting the sea. Chalky rock deposited in shallow, warm prehistoric seas is also rich in flint nodules, from which many houses and churches in the area are built. The Weald, further inland, is a series of ridged valleys formed through millions of years of erosion, and is heavily forested.

Sussex has seen some of the most significant moments in British history, and has been home to many famous writers and artists. Some of the rides take in the home villages of authors Anthony Trollope and Hilaire Belloc. Pop Larkin's creator H.E. Bates was stationed at RAF Tangmere, now a museum of aviation. Edward Elgar composed his famous cello concerto while living near Fittleworth, and A.A. Milne was inspired to set the Winnie-the-Pooh and Christopher Robin stories in Ashdown Forest.

Piltdown was the site of a famous fraud, when ambitious scientists claimed to have found the earliest human remains in a gravel pit. In fact all they had were stained animal bones. But Sussex got its own back with the discovery of Boxgrove Man, whose remains have been dated at around 400,000 years old.

Bodiam Castle (see Route 21)

Boxgrove Man was the first of a succession of colonists in Sussex. Neolithic colonists mined the Downs for flints, and relics of Bronze Age life and death can be seen in forts, dykes and burial mounds throughout the Downs. The Romans arrived in AD43 and established the thriving town of Chichester, coastal defences and scattered villas throughout the countryside. The Romans gave way to the Saxons, who established a separate kingdom, which survived until the Norman Conquest of 1066, when the invading French beat the British defenders at the Battle of Hastings. Many Sussex names have Norman French derivations.

Sussex became the Sheffield of the south as an iron-producing area in the 15th century, with the inland Weald forests being felled to provide fuel and charcoal for smelting metal, founding a thriving armaments industry. Many of the county's castles were sieged, attacked and some all but demolished in the English Civil War, where the local business – making weapons – made Sussex a place of great strategic importance. The Spanish Armada passed within sight of the Sussex coast on its way to ruin, and there are reports of Sir Francis Drake complaining at being fired on by guns made in Sussex after a naval battle with the Spanish. The last foundry was closed by the early 1800s, and the largely agricultural Sussex economy that exists today began to form.

Preparing for a cycling trip

Basic maintenance

A cycle ride is an immense pleasure, particularly on a warm sunny day. Nothing is better than coasting along a country lane gazing over the countryside. Unfortunately, not every cycling day is as perfect as this, and it is important to make sure that your bike is in good order and that you are taking the necessary clothing and supplies with you.

Before you go out on your bicycle check that everything is in order. Pump the tyres up if needed, and check that the brakes are working properly and that nothing is loose – the brakes are the only means of stopping quickly and safely. If there is a problem and you are not sure that you can fix it, take the bike to a cycle repair shop – they can often deal with small repairs very quickly.

When you go out cycling it is important to take either a puncture repair kit or a spare inner tube – it is often quicker to replace the inner tube in the event of a puncture, though it may be a good idea to practise first. You also need a pump, and with a slow puncture the pump may be enough to get you home. To remove the tyre you need a set of tyre levers. Other basic tools are an Allen key and a spanner. Some wheels on modern bikes can be removed by quick release levers built into the bike. Take a lock for your bike and if you have to leave it at any time, leave it in public view and locked through the frame and front wheel to something secure.

What to wear and take with you

It is not necessary to buy specialised cycling clothes. If it is not warm enough to wear shorts wear trousers which are easy to move in but fairly close to the leg below the knee – leggings are ideal – as this stops the trousers catching the chain. If you haven't got narrow-legged trousers, bicycle clips will hold them in. Jeans are not a good idea as they are rather tight and difficult to cycle in, and if they get wet they take a long time to dry. If your shorts or trousers are thin you might get a bit sore from being too long on the saddle. This problem can be reduced by using a gel saddle, and by wearing thicker, or extra, pants. Once you are a committed cyclist you can buy cycling shorts; or undershorts which have a protective pad built in and which can be worn under anything. It is a good idea to wear several thin layers of clothes so that you can add or remove layers as necessary. A zip-fronted top gives easy temperature control. Make sure you have something warm and something waterproof.

If you wear shoes with a firm, flat sole you will be able to exert pressure on the pedals easily, and will have less work to do to make the bicycle move. Gloves not only keep your hands warm but protect them in the event that you come off, and cycling mittens which cushion your hands are not expensive. A helmet is not a legal requirement, but it will protect your head if you fall.

In general it is a good idea to wear bright clothing so that you can be easily seen by motorists, and this is particularly important when it is overcast or getting dark. If you might be out in the dark or twilight fit your bicycle with lights – by law your bicycle must have a reflector. You can also buy reflective bands for your ankles, or to wear over your shoulder and back, and these help motorists to see you.

You may be surprised how quickly you use up energy when cycling, and it is important to eat a carbohydrate meal before you set out. When planning a long ride, eat well the night before. You should eat small amounts of food regularly while you are cycling, or you may find that your energy suddenly disappears, particularly if there are hills or if the weather is cold. It is important to always carry something to eat with you – chocolate, bananas, biscuits – so that if you do start fading away you can restore yourself quickly. In warm weather you will sweat and use up fluid, and you always need to carry something to drink – water will do! Many bicycles have a fitment in which to put a water bottle, and if you don't have one a cycle shop should be able to fit one.

It is also a good idea to carry a small first aid kit. This should include elastoplasts or bandages, sunburn cream, and an anti-histamine in case you are stung by a passing insect.

It is a good idea to have a pannier to carry all these items. Some fit on the handlebars, some to the back of the seat and some onto a back rack. For a day's ride you probably won't need a lot of carrying capacity, but it is better to carry items in a pannier rather than in a rucksack on your back. Pack items that you are carrying carefully – loose items can be dangerous.

Getting to the start of the ride

If you are lucky you will be able to cycle to the start of the ride, but often transport is necessary. If you travel there by train, some sprinter services carry two bicycles without prior booking. Other services carry bicycles free in off-peak periods, but check the details with your local station. Alternatively, you could use your car – it may be possible to get a bike in the back of a hatchback if you take out the front wheel. There are inexpensive, easily fitted car racks which carry bicycles safely. Your local cycle store will be able to supply one to suit you.

Cycling on-road

Cycling on back roads is a delight with quiet lanes, interesting villages, good views and a smooth easy surface to coast along on. The cycle rides in this book are mainly on quiet roads but you sometimes cross busy roads or have stretches on B roads, and whatever sort of road you are on it is essential to ride safely. Always be aware of the possibility or existence of other traffic. Glance behind regularly, signal before you turn or change lane, and keep to the left. If there are motorists around, make sure that they have seen you before you cross their path. Cycling can be dangerous if you are

The Long Man of Wilmington on the South Downs Way (see Routes 12 and 25)

competing for space with motor vehicles, many of which seem to have difficulty in seeing cyclists. When drivers are coming out of side roads, catch their eye before you ride in front of them.

You will find that many roads have potholes and uneven edges. They are much more difficult to spot when you are in a group because of the restricted view ahead, and therefore warnings need to be given. It is a good idea to cycle about a metre out into the road, conditions permitting, so that you avoid the worst of the uneven surfaces and to give you room to move in·to the left if you are closely overtaken by a motor vehicle.

Other things to be careful of are slippery roads, particularly where there is mud or fallen leaves. Sudden rain after a period of dry weather often makes the roads extremely slippery. Dogs, too, are a hazard because they often move unpredictably, and sometimes like to chase cyclists. If you are not happy, stop or go slowly until the problem has passed.

Pedalling

Many modern bikes have 18 or 21 gears with three rings at the front and six or seven on the back wheel, and for much of the time you will find that the middle gear at the front with the range of gears at the back will be fine. Use your gears to find one that is easy to pedal along in so that your feet move round easily and you do not put too much pressure on your knees. If you are new to the bike and the gears it is a good idea to practise changing the gears on a stretch of flat, quiet road so that when you need to change gears quickly you will be ready to do so.

Cycling in a group

When cycling in a group it is essential to do so in a disciplined manner for your own, and others', safety. Do not ride too close to the bicycle in front of you – keep about a bicycle's length between you so that you will have space to brake or stop. Always keep both hands on the handlebars, except when signalling, etc. It is alright to cycle two abreast on quiet roads, but if it is necessary to change from cycling two abreast to single file this is usually done by the outside rider falling in behind the nearside rider; always cycle in single file where there are double white lines, on busy roads, or on narrow and winding roads where you have a restricted view of the road ahead. Overtake on the right (outside) only; do not overtake on the inside.

It is important to pass information to other members of the group, for example:

car up – a vehicle is coming up behind the group and will be overtaking;

car down – a vehicle is coming towards the group;

single up – get into single file;

stopping – stopping, or

slowing/easy – slowing due to junction, etc., ahead;

on the left – there is an obstacle on the left, e.g. pedestrian, parked car;

pothole – pothole (and point towards it).

Accidents

In case of an accident, stay calm and, if needed, ring the emergency services on 999. It is a good idea to carry a basic first aid kit and perhaps also one of the commercial foil wraps to put around anyone who has an accident to keep them warm. If someone comes off their bicycle move them and the bike off the road if it is safe to do so. Get someone in the party to warn approaching traffic to slow down, and if necessary ring for an ambulance.

Cycling off-road

All the routes in this book take you along legal rights of way – bridleways, byways open to all traffic and roads used as public paths – it is illegal to cycle along footpaths. Generally the off-road sections of the routes will be easy if the weather and ground are dry. If the weather has been wet and the ground is muddy, it is not a good idea to cycle along bridleways unless you do not mind getting dirty and unless you have a mountain bike which will not get blocked up with mud. In dry weather any bicycle will be able to cover the bridleway sections, but you may need to dismount if the path is very uneven.

Off-road cycling is different to cycling on the road. The average speed is lower, you will use more energy, your riding style will be different and there is a different set of rules to obey – the off-road code:

1   Give way to horse riders and pedestrians, and use a bell or call out to warn someone of your presence.

2   Take your rubbish with you.

3   Do not light fires.

4   Close gates behind you.

5   Do not interfere with wildlife, plants or trees.

6   Use only tracks where you have a right of way, or where the landowner has given you permission to ride.

7   Avoid back wheel skids, which can start erosion gulleys and ruin the bridleway.

Some of the off-road rides take you some miles from shelter and civilisation – take waterproofs, plenty of food and drink and basic tools – especially spare inner-tubes, and tyre repair equipment. Tell someone where you are going and approximately when you are due back. You are more likely to tumble off your bike riding off-road, so you should consider wearing a helmet and mittens with padded palms.

Local Tourist Information Centres

Battle
88 High Street, Battle
Telephone (01424) 773721

Bognor Regis
Bemont Street, Bognor Regis
Telephone (01243) 823140

Boship
Lower Dicker, Hailsham
Telephone (01323) 442667

Brighton
10 Bartholomew Square, Brighton
Telephone (01273) 323755

Chichester
29a South Street, Chichester
Telephone (01243) 775888

Eastbourne
Cornfield Road, Eastbourne
Telephone (01323) 411400

Guildford
14 Tunsgate, Guildford
Telephone (01483) 444007

Lewes
187 High Street, Lewes
Telephone (01273) 483448

Petersfield
Country Library, 27 The Square, Petersfield
Telephone (01730) 268829

Petworth
Market Square, Petworth
Telephone (01798) 343523

Pevensey
Pevensey Castle, High Street, Pevensey
Telephone (01323) 761444

Local cycle hire

Castle Cycle Hire
Hailsham
Telephone (01323) 833537

Cuckmere Cycle Co Ltd
High Street, Horam
Telephone (01435) 813000

Seven Sisters Country Park
Seaford
Telephone (01323) 870310

Bewl Water
Lamberhurst
Telephone (0860) 3865144

Local cycle shops

Cycle Revival
Hailsham Road, Heathfield
Telephone (01435) 866118

Chris Pelling Motor Store
High Street, Hailsham
Telephone (01323) 840601

Sensible Bicycle Company
Station Road, Liss
Telephone (01730) 894884

SINGLETON MUSEUM TO GOODWOOD AND THE TRUNDLE

Route information

Distance 15km (9.5 miles)

Grade Moderate

Terrain Quiet, well-maintained Sussex lanes, with some climbs towards the end of the route. Suitable for most bikes, and for families with children of 11 upwards.

Time to allow 1-3 hours.

Getting there by car The ride starts at the Weald and Downland Open Air Museum, off the A286 Chichester to Haslemere road, and parking is available at the museum.

Getting there by train The closest station is Chichester, connected with London Victoria and on the Portsmouth to Brighton line, telephone (0345) 484950 for enquiries. Singleton is 9km (5.5 miles) up the A286. Alternatively, leave Chichester on the A285 (SP Petworth) and start the route at direction 7 (Woodcote).

From the Weald and Downland Open Air Museum on a short loop through quiet lanes and a site of great archaeological interest – this short ride merits a moderate grade because it involves several short but steady climbs. The lanes are mixed – some hemmed in by woodland on either side, some with open views to the top of the South Downs and across the sea. It is a good introduction to dealing with

hills sensibly on a bike – get the whole family in low gears and winch your way up.

Places of interest along the route

A Weald and Downland Open Air Museum, Singleton, Chichester

Twenty hectares (50 acres) of Sussex history and heritage, with over 40 historic buildings that have been rescued from destruction and restored. There is a medieval farmstead, a working water-powered flour mill, a Victorian rural school as well as farm livestock, demonstrations of building crafts and countryside skills and a quiet picnic area. This is a compulsory stop. Open daily from March to October 1100-1800, and on Wednesdays, Saturdays and Sundays through the winter 1100-1600 (except between 26 December and 3 January). Charge. Telephone (01243) 811348.

B Goodwood House and Country Park, Goodwood, Chichester

The Country Park comprises 24 hectares (60 acres) of mixed woodland and chalky Downs grassland, next to the famous glorious Goodwood racecourse. With space for peaceful walks, there are picturesque picnic sites and views to the sea. Goodwood House, country home of the Dukes of Richmond and Gordon since 1697, is open to the public on most Sunday and Monday afternoons (1400-1700) between April and September and contains paintings by Canaletto, Van Dyck, Stubbs and Reynolds, rare French furniture and tapestries, and a priceless collection of Sèvres porcelain. Charge. Goodwood House is sometimes closed for special events so telephone (01243) 774107 to check opening times in advance of your visit.

ⓒ The Trundle,
Goodwood, Chichester

The site of an ancient hill top fort, over 2000 years old. The earthworks – ditches and ramparts – are still visible. The area is covered by a network of public paths and, when the skies are clear, there are tremendous views over the south coast.

Food and drink

Refreshments are available along the route: the Weald and Downland Open Air Museum serves refreshments in a timber-framed medieval hall; cream teas are served at Goodwood House; there is also a picnic area at Goodwood Country Park.

Horse and Groom, Singleton

A pub on the A286 which is used to tourists and welcomes children at lunchtimes. Food available lunchtimes and evenings (except Wednesday to Sunday evenings in winter).

Hurdlemakers, East Dean

A one-stop refreshment service – pub and village shop in one, with beer garden, separate family room, lunchtime and evening meals, and bed and breakfast.

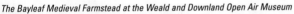

The Bayleaf Medieval Farmstead at the Weald and Downland Open Air Museum

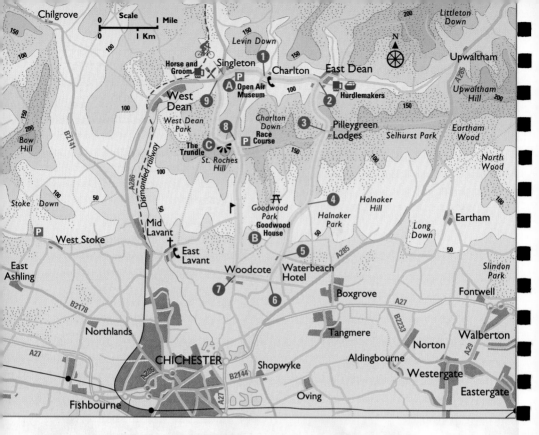

Route description 🚴

Leave the museum, turn right off the A286 SP Charlton and East Dean.

1 Arrive Charlton, SO to East Dean.

2 Arrive at East Dean XR, TR.

3 Arrive Pilleygreen Lodges, SO at XR.

4 Road bears right. **5.5km (3.5 miles)**

5 Pass Waterbeach. Goodwood Park can be seen on the right.

6 Arrive XR, TR.

7 Arrive XR, TR again. **9km (5.5 miles)**

8 TL SP The Trundle, then follow this road around a right-angle bend and return to the A286, and the Open Air Museum.

9 Finish the ride at the museum, not forgetting the nearby Horse and Groom pub.

15km (9.5 miles)

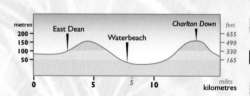

THE CUCKOO TRAIL – POLEGATE TO HEATHFIELD

Route information

Distance 17.5km (11 miles) one way

Grade Easy

Terrain Flat, traffic-free track, some of which is tarmacked, with short sections of road. Ideal family cycling and suitable for any type of bicycle.

Time to allow 1-3 hours, depending on speed.

Getting there by car Polegate is on the A27 Pevensey to Brighton road and there is car parking at Polegate Station.

Getting there by train Polegate Station is on the Brighton-Eastbourne-Ashford line. For timetable enquiries telephone (0345) 484950. There are no rail links to return you to the start point, so this can be a there-and-back-again ride; alternatively, simply turn back when you are ready.

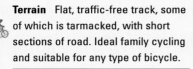

From Polegate to Heathfield along the Cuckoo Trail, one of the many tracks that came from Dr Beeching's famous axing of railway lines throughout Britain. It is ideal for a leisurely family ride, fully signposted, with benches, sculptures and opportunities for food and drink throughout the ride.

Places of interest along the route

Ⓐ The Cuckoo Trail

The Cuckoo Trail is of interest itself. The derelict track bed of the former Eastbourne to Hailsham line is now part of the National Cycle Network, built by the local authority and the charity Sustrans. The Cuckoo Line was opened in 1849 and was well-used until the 1960s. The last passenger train ran in 1968. As a rural railway it was not only passengers that made the journey – milk, livestock and animal feed were also carried. Railway workers first coined the name 'Cuckoo' after local tradition that the first cuckoo of spring was released at Heathfield fair. The trail is waymarked with large milestone sculptures, and dotted with benches carved out of oak trees that were felled during the 1987 storms. There are plans to extend the route in future years, as part of the 2000-mile long National Cycle Network millennium project. The Cuckoo Trail has its own code of conduct for cyclists (which of course would apply to any similar track): give way to walkers, horses and people with disabilities; always sound your bell when approaching walkers; always leave ample room when passing other users; slow down at bends; cycle carefully and responsibly. For further information on the Cuckoo Trail, contact either Boship Tourist Information Centre on (01323) 442667 or Pevensey Tourist Information Centre on (01323) 761444.

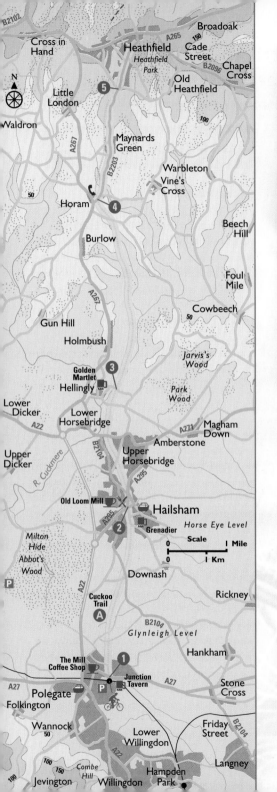

Food and drink

🍺 **Junction Tavern, Polegate**
Close to the Cuckoo Trail start. Real ale, open fires, midday and evening meals.

☕ **The Mill Coffee Shop, Polegate**
Coffee shop offering light refreshments.

🍺 **Grenadier, Hailsham**
Popular with Cuckoo Trail walkers and cyclists.

🍺 **Golden Martlet, Hellingly**
Garden. Children are welcome.

☕ **The Old Loom Mill, Mulbrooks Farm,**
✗ **Ersham Road, Hailsham**
Tea, coffee and lunch next to the route.

Route description

1 Leave Polegate Station TR. At TJ with A27 TR then first left into School Lane, and the trail entrance is ahead of you as the road bends left.

2 Arrive Hailsham. The trail kinks right into Station Road for a short road link which turns left then sharp right to continue through Hailsham centre, after passing under London Road. The trail joins a further short road link (The Cedars) and leaves Hailsham.
5km (3 miles)

3 The trail passes Hellingly.

4 Arrive Horam.

5 Arrive Heathfield, where the trail finishes in Station Road. **17.5km (11 miles)**

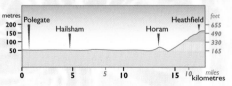

Route 3

ALFRISTON VILLAGE AND DRUSILLAS PARK ZOO

Route information

 Distance 18.5km (11.5 miles)

Grade Moderate

Terrain All the roads encountered on this route are good tarmac, but like much of Sussex there are some hills to tackle. Suitable for most types of bicycle, although bikes should have low gears for hill climbing. Children of 13 and over will be able to do this ride comfortably.

Time to allow Around 2 hours, but there is plenty to stop and see, so allow more time.

Getting there by car Alfriston is off the A27 Lewes to Eastbourne Road, with limited parking at Alfriston, and parking at Drusillas Park, which features on the ride.

Getting there by train Berwick Station is on the Burgess Hill to Eastbourne line. For timetable information telephone (0345) 484950. Bicycles are carried free at off-peak hours (after 0930 Monday to Friday, throughout the day at weekends), subject to space being available.

This route travels from Alfriston village to Drusillas Park and then on to Michelham Priory. Alfriston lies in a gap cut in the eastern end of the South Downs by the Cuckmere River, and is the start point of an undemanding ride through *undulating scenery offering excellent views inland and over Seaford to the Channel. Alfriston is one of the most charming villages in the Downs, with houses built out of local sandstone and flint. Besides interesting cycling, the ride passes Drusillas Park, one of the finest and most accessible zoos in the south of England.*

Places of interest along the route

Ⓐ Drusillas Park, Alfriston

Drusillas Park is well worth a visit, and should hold you up for some time, especially if you have children with you. Described as the best small zoo in the country, there are plenty of animals in well-designed habitats. Trains running through farm paddocks, an outdoor playground and a try-it-yourself artificial cow to milk are among the attractions. There are also beautiful gardens, a garden shop, pottery workshop and gift shop. Refreshments are available. Open daily throughout the year (except for 24, 25 and 26 December) from 1000 with last admission at 1700 in summer and at 1600 in winter. Charge for the zoo only. Telephone (01323) 870234.

Ⓑ Michelham Priory, Upper Dicker, Hailsham

Michelham Priory is a beautiful, peaceful stop surrounded by England's longest medieval water-filled moat. An imposing 14th-century gatehouse can still be seen, together with the lines of the priory and church, dissolved by Henry VIII in 1537. There are gardens to wander through and exhibits, housed in a Tudor building, to browse over. Also on the site is a smithy, wheelwright's shop, museum of rope-making and a water mill. Refreshments are available and there is a picnic area and children's playground. The priory is open on Wednesdays through to Sundays and on Bank Holiday Mondays between March and October (daily in August). Opening times are March and October 1100-1600, April-July and September 1100-1700. Charge. Telephone (01323) 844224.

C Alfriston Clergy House, Alfriston

Alfriston Clergy House is a thatched 14th-century Wealden Hall House and, in 1896, was the first building bought by the National Trust. A medieval hall and several rooms are open to the public. There is a charming cottage garden containing many rare plants and giving views of the Cuckmere River. The house is open daily between March and October 1030-1700 (or sunset if earlier). Charge. Telephone (01323) 870001.

Food and drink

Alfriston is a popular tourist spot, and there are too many quaint cafés to list. Refreshments are also available at Drusillas Park where there is a restaurant/café and a pub, and at Michelham Priory which has tearooms and a restaurant.

Star Inn, Alfriston
Low beamed ceilings, real ale and an old-world atmosphere. A distinctive red lion carving stands outside this pub.

Plough and Harrow, Litlington
An excellent watering hole towards the end of the ride, with a beer garden and food served at lunchtimes and evening.

Alfriston Clergy House

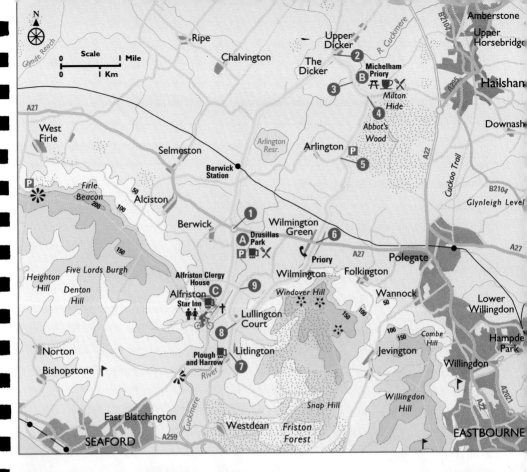

Route description

Leave Alfriston north to Berwick and A27.

1 XR with A27, Drusillas Park is signed on your right as you approach the XR. After leaving Drusillas, cross A27 heading for Berwick Station, over the level crossing, SO.

2 TR to Milton Hide. *4.5km (3 miles)*

3 Pass Michelham Priory on the left.

4 Arrive Milton Hide TR.

5 TL direction Wilmington. *9km (5.5 miles)*

6 Arrive XR with A27, SO through Wilmington Green, pass Wilmington Priory (not open to public) on the left.

7 Continue to Litlington 16km (10 miles) for the Plough and Harrow PH. About turn and leave the village by the road you entered until:

8 TL at Lullington Court. *17.5km (11 miles)*

9 A further 0.5km on TL across the Cuckmere River, then left again to end the ride in Alfriston. *18.5km (11.5 miles)*

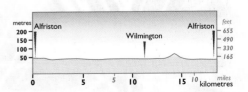

SELSEY BILL – A SHORT, FLAT TOUR BY THE SEA

Route information

Distance 22 km (13.5 miles)

Grade Easy

Terrain This ride is on Selsey Bill, a flat headland that sticks into the English Channel. The ride is suitable for families and within the capability of bicycles with few gears.

Time to allow 2 hours.

Getting there by car Bosham is on the A27 between Chichester and Havant, with parking in Bosham village.

Getting there by train Bosham Station can be reached from Havant and Chichester Stations. Havant is on the Waterloo-Portsmouth line, change at Havant for Bosham. Trains from Brighton stop at Bosham. Telephone (0345) 484950 for timetable information. You can catch the train from Chichester to Bosham at the end of the ride.

This rides leaves from Bosham Station, taking in villages on Selsey Bill, and finishes at historic Chichester. A flat, easy ride that should only be avoided if the weather forecast predicts strong winds, since the terrain is flat and a stiff wind off the sea can make riding hard work. The route offers excellent views over Chichester Harbour, and you may wish to pack binoculars, since the harbour mud flats have a thriving colony of wading and sea birds. A short ferry trip from Bosham to West Itchenor breaks the ride up. Note that the ferry operates between April and September at weekends and daily during the school holidays. Ring Chichester Tourist Information Centre on (01243) 775888 for further details. At other times of the year treat this as a there-and-back-again ride, starting at West Itchenor (direction 3) and riding as far as you like towards Chichester, before turning back. The Romans made Chichester one of their main administrative centres in the south, and Fishbourne Roman Palace (to the west of Chichester) is an interesting diversion. See Route 7 for details. Bird watchers not sated by Chichester Harbour may wish to detour to Pagham Harbour.

Route description

Leave Bosham station onto the B2146, TL

1 At the roundabout, SO.

2 Arrive TJ in Bosham, TR into the village and follow road parallel to the coast.

3 Arrive at the ferry to West Itchenor, and after disembarking, SO through the village. Keep right through the village of Shipton Green.

4 Arrive at XR with the B2179 SO to continue the route, or TR for the Lamb PH.

5km (3 miles)

5 Arrive East Wittering (shops here) TJ, TL.

6 TL onto B2198 (10km, 6 miles) then watch out for:

7 TR to Earnley.

8 Road forks, bear right through Almodington.

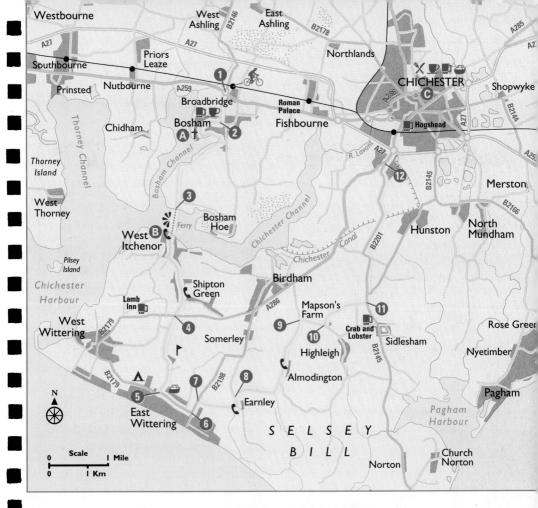

9 TR towards Sidlesham. **15km (9.5 miles)**

10 TL at Mapson's Farm.

11 TJ with B2145, TL then take left fork up B2201 SP Chichester. For the Crab and Lobster PH at Sidlesham, TR along B2145 for 300m (328 yards).

12 At TJ with A286, TR into Chichester, SO at the roundabout, arriving at Chichester Station. Straight on across the ring road (Avenue des Chartres and Market Avenue) into South Street for the Hogshead pub.

22km (13.5 miles)

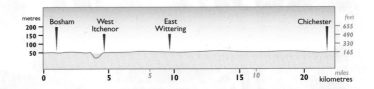

Places of interest along the route

A Bosham

A National Trust site, Bosham contributed the name to Lord Bosham, the Earl of Emsworth's dim-witted son in P.G. Wodehouse's famous series of books about Blandings Castle.

B West Itchenor

This village offers spectacular views over the estimated 1619 hectares (4000 acres) of Chichester Harbour, an Area of Outstanding Natural Beauty. If you want a break, a 1½ hour boat trip around the harbour runs from West Itchenor. Weather permitting, the boat trips run all year round, but telephone (01243) 786418 to confirm times before you turn up.

C Chichester

Attractions include the cathedral, started in the 11th century, Chichester District Museum (located in the city centre) and the nearby Guildhall Museum, where the poet William Blake once stood trial on charges of sedition.

Food and drink

There is a selection of pubs and tearooms to try in Bosham, should you have an appetite this early in the ride. The route passes shops in East Wittering too. Chichester offers the usual range of pubs, restaurants and cafés expected in such a city.

Lamb Inn, West Wittering
A short diversion off the route along the B2179 at direction 4. A quiet pub with a good range of beers and a large menu, served lunchtimes and evenings except Sunday evenings in winter.

Crab and Lobster, Sidlesham
This pub offers open fires, CAMRA-commended beers and an attractive garden.

Hogshead, 50 South Street, Chichester
Close to the station, this pub is reputed for its moderately priced food and its immodest selection of real ales – 11 of them.

Bosham, on Chichester Harbour

BENTLEY WILDLIFE AND MOTOR MUSEUM

Route information

Distance 25.5km (16 miles)

Grade Moderate

Terrain Much of the ride is on the Sussex coastal plain, so there are few hills and well-surfaced roads. Suitable for all types of road bike and all-terrain bikes.

Time to allow 2-4 hours.

Getting there by car Berwick is on the A27 Lewes to Eastbourne road with parking in the village and at Drusillas Park.

Getting there by train Berwick Station is served by Connex South Central who allow free bicycle carriage off-peak. For further information telephone (0345) 484950. This ride is not a loop. However, the finishing point at Glynde Station is just one stop from Berwick, the starting point.

From Berwick to the Bentley Wildfowl and Motor Museum, and on to Glynde, this route is ideal for a family ride, since it is mostly level and has not only a museum but a wildfowl centre and zoo. Car fans, naturalists, and historians will find plenty to interest them on this ride. The route also passes close to the famous Glyndebourne opera house.

Places of interest along the route

Ⓐ Bentley Wildfowl and Motor Museum, Halland, near Lewes

The Bentley Wildfowl and Motor Museum contains over 115 species of wildfowl as well as gardens, picnic area and a motor museum. Open daily from March to October, from 1030 with last admissions at 1630 (1700 in July and August) and during the winter open at weekends only, from 1030 with last admissions at 1600. Charge. Telephone (01825) 840573.

Ⓑ Drusillas Park, Alfriston

Drusillas Park makes a pleasant end to the ride on your return to Berwick, especially if you have children with you. There are plenty of animals in well-designed habitats and close contact with the birds and animals in various exhibits. The park also contains farm paddocks, an outdoor playground and a try-it-yourself artificial cow to milk. There are gardens, a garden shop, pottery workshop and gift shop. Open daily from 1000 with last admission at 1700 in summer and at 1600 in winter. Charge for entry to the zoo. Telephone (01323) 870234.

Food and drink

Both the Bentley Estate and Drusillas Park offer light refreshments.

Ⓒ Cricketer's Arms, Berwick
A quiet pub with open fires and lunchtime and evening meals.

Route description

Leave Berwick, cross the A27 in the direction of Berwick Station and Arlington Reservoir.

1 Cross Berwick Station level crossing.

2 After a good view of Arlington Reservoir, TL.

3 TR into narrow road leading to Laughton.
5km (3 miles)

4 SP Laughton TL along this twisting road – beware oncoming cars.

5 XR with the B2124, SO. *11km (7 miles)*

6 Arrive at the TJ with B2192, TL.

7 TR off B2192 and right again to the Bentley Wildfowl and Motor Museum.
15.5km (9.5 miles)

8 After leaving museum, TL to rejoin route.

9 Arrive at the TJ with the B2192, TR.
22km (13.5 miles)

10 TL off B2192, then arrive at TJ with B2124, TL then first right following signposts to Glynde.

11 After a stretch of road with excellent views over the ridge of the South Downs, finish the ride at Glynde Station. *25.5 km (16 miles)*

The South Downs, near Alfriston

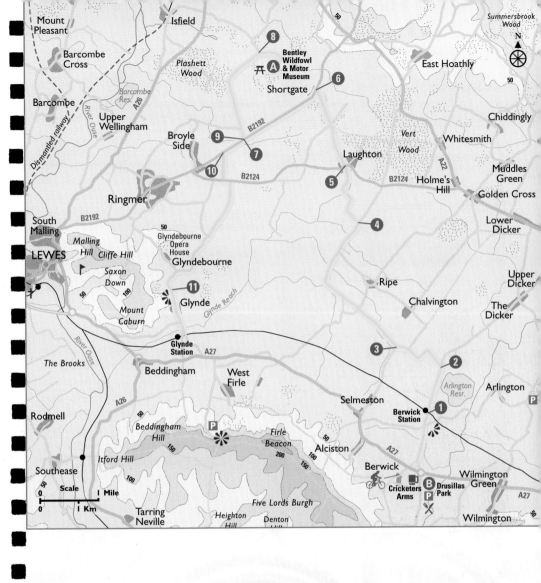

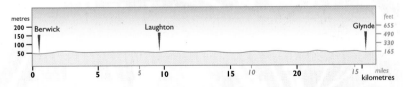

AMBERLEY TO SHOREHAM ON THE SOUTH DOWNS WAY

Route information

 Distance 25.5km (16 miles)

Grade Strenuous

Terrain This route's terrain is mostly off-road, on well-defined tracks that include hard, dry, bumpy tracks, sometimes strewn with tree roots and loose rocks. It is suitable for all-terrain bikes, and can be tackled by older teenagers. This route gets very boggy after rain.

Time to allow Up to 3 hours.

Getting there by car Amberley is on the B2139, off the A29 Bognor Regis road. There is parking in and around the village.

Getting there by train Amberley Station is on the Littlehampton to Crawley line, telephone (0345) 484950 for timetable information. The ride finishes at Shoreham-by-Sea, where you can catch a train to Littlehampton, changing at Littlehampton to return to the start of the ride at Amberley Station.

This is a ride in the real South Downs, on the well-defined South Downs Way that runs along the crest of the hills. The views are spectacular and the riding is entertaining, with some steep climbs and long, fast descents. The South Downs Way avoids towns and villages and there are no opportunities for refreshments along the track itself. Although this is a relatively short ride, off-road cycling is energetic, so take plenty of snacks and drinks with you. If your bike does get clogged with mud after this ride, hose it off and relubricate it when you get home – this is gritty mud and destructive to a bike's moving parts.

Places of interest along the route

A Amberley Museum, Amberley, near Arundel

Amberley is strikingly beautiful with its 12th-century church and castle dominating the village (the castle is not open to the public). Amberley Museum is sited in a former chalk quarry, adjacent to Amberley Station. The museum features many examples of industries that supported the local economy in the past, such as blacksmiths, wheelwrights, broom makers, boat builders and road makers. There are steam vehicles, a vintage wireless exhibition, lime kilns and rides can be taken on a vintage motor bus or a narrow gauge railway. The 14.5 hectare (36 acre site) also includes a nature trail and excellent picnic areas. The museum is open between late March and October, Wednesdays to Sundays, plus Bank Holidays, from 1000-1700 and daily during school holidays. Charge. Telephone for details on (01798) 831370.

B Chanctonbury Ring, on the South Downs Way

This site has been home to an Iron Age fort and a Roman temple, but now a vestigial, distinctive circular bank remains. It was cloaked in trees until the 1987 storm flattened many of them, and saplings have been planted to ultimately restore the site to its former tree-covered glory.

C Steyning Museum, Church Street, Steyning

The museum features many displays of the history of Steyning, from Saxon times up to the present day, and is much visited by walkers and cyclists passing through the area. A changing exhibition concentrates on particular areas of Steyning's history. The museum is open all year round in the mornings on Tuesdays, Wednesdays, Fridays and Saturdays between 1030 and 1230; in the afternoons from April to September between 1400 and 1630; in the afternoons from October to March between 1430 and 1600. Free entry. For further details telephone (01903) 813333.

D Marlipins Museum, High Street, Shoreham-by-Sea

Marlipins is managed by the Shoreham Society on behalf of the Sussex Archaeological Society. The building itself is of Norman origin and is thought once to have been a customs house. It has a wonderful chequer-work façade of knapped flints and Caen stone. The museum contains exhibits on maritime history and local history as far back as man's earliest occupation of the area. The museum is open between May and September, Tuesdays to Saturdays, 1000-1300 and 1400-1630, Sundays 1400-1600. Charge. Telephone (01273) 462994.

Steyning

Food and drink

There are pubs and teashops to choose from in Amberley and a café at the museum. Shoreham has the usual shops you would expect from a town of this size, and pubs for food and drink.

Chequers, High Street, Steyning
Good beer and lunchtime and evening meals in a building that dates from the 15th century.

Marlipins, High Street, Shoreham-by-Sea
A quiet pub with lunchtime and evening meals, close to the railway station.

Lazy Toad, High Street, Shoreham-by-Sea
Pub serving food at lunchtimes only. Beer comes from the barrels on display behind the counter.

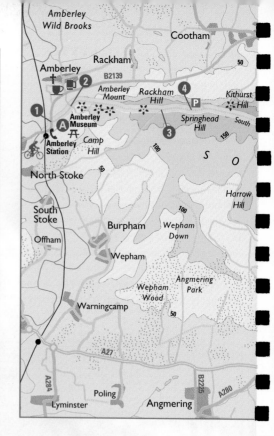

Route description

Leave Amberley Station and turn left onto the B2139.

1 Turn right into High Titton Lane.

2 Within 100m (328 feet), arrive at a TJ and bear right then TL onto the South Downs Way (SDW), clearly signed up Amberley Mount. Start climbing towards Rackham Hill, noticing burial barrows on each side of the track.

3 Arrive Rackham Hill, continue along the route to Springhead Hill.

4 Pass car park at Springhead Hill, continue eastwards, as the SDW turns into surfaced track. Note that there is a tap on the right of the lane. **4.5km (3 miles)**

5 After a furious descent, arrive XR with A24, straight across.

6 Arrive Chanctonbury Ring. After visiting this ancient site, continue eastwards along the SDW. **11.5km (7 miles)**

7 SDW joins a small, single-track lane, TL and descend towards Steyning.

8 Arrive Steyning centre, with the museum immediately opposite. TR to continue the route, pass a church on your right, then third road on the right, TR towards Botolphs. **15.5km (9.5 miles)**

9 At Botolphs Church TL through gateway onto the Downs Link track, along the track to the riverside, bear right and cross the bridges over the River Adur. **19km (12 miles)**

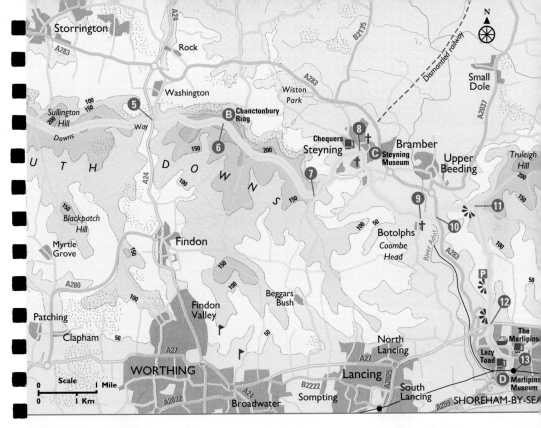

10 TL and cross the A283 (careful – it's busy) and TL for 120m (394 feet) parallel to the road, then before the roundabout TR to rejoin the SDW.

11 TR off the SDW towards Shoreham-by-Sea.

12 Bridge over the A27, ride into Shoreham-by-Sea, and at TJ TL into town Centre.

13 Ride ends at Shoreham Station.

25.5km (16 miles)

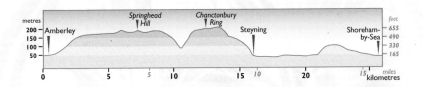

FISHBOURNE TO CHICHESTER – A RIDE THROUGH HISTORY

Route information

Distance 28.5km (17.5 miles)

Grade Easy

Terrain Suitable for everyone, since this ride runs along the flat Chichester coastal plain with a short dip into the Lavant Valley north of Chichester.

Time to allow 1-3 hours.

Getting there by car Fishbourne is easily accessible from the A27 Havant to Chichester road, with pay-and-display parking in Fishbourne. This is a busy tourist area and parking can be difficult during school holidays.

Getting there by train Fishbourne Station is on the Portsmouth to Brighton line (Connex South Central) and the London Waterloo to Portsmouth line (South West Trains) stops at Havant, where you change for Fishbourne. Telephone (0345) 484950 for information. The ride finishes in Chichester and Fishbourne is less than two miles along the A27. However, you may wish to avoid riding down the busy A27 to return to your car by catching the train from Chichester Station one stop to Fishbourne.

This rides goes from Fishbourne on the outskirts of Chichester, taking in the Chichester coastal plain, Lavant Valley and Boxgrove and has a strong Roman flavour – Chichester was the Roman settlement of Noviomagus, and the ride starts near the Roman Palace at Fishbourne. Further evidence of Roman domination of the area can be seen in Sane Street, the Roman road that runs northeast from Chichester following the line of the A285, that you will cross part-way through the ride. Italian invaders may have dominated the area for more than three centuries, but the ride also passes Boxgrove, site of the earliest human settlement in Britain, and Tangmere, where modern Britons fought the Battle of Britain to stop Britain succumbing to invasion from across the Channel. The route also passes close to Goodwood House and Country Park (see Route 2 for details).

Places of interest along the route

Ⓐ Fishbourne Roman Palace, Fishbourne, near Chichester

The Roman Palace is at the start of the ride, and is thought to be the most extensive Roman building yet discovered in Britain. Only the north wing is visible and mosaics and remains of corridors, hypocausts (heating systems), a bath suite and other artefacts can be seen. The east and west wings were excavated then reburied. The Romans were great road builders, so it is ironic that the south wing of this massive palace is thought to have been entombed when the A259 was built.

The site also has a Museum of Roman Gardening, displaying a wide range of herbs, vines, vegetables and fruit grown in Roman times. Open from March to July and September to October 1000-1700; August 1000-1800; November to February 1000-1600. Opening times shown are daily throughout the year, except mid-December to mid-February, when the palace is open on Sundays only. Charge. Telephone (01243) 785859.

B Boxgrove Priory,
Boxgrove, near Chichester

The priory was built in the 12th century by the Benedictines, the first Christian monastic order. Predictably, the Priory suffered during the dissolution of the monasteries following the Reformation, and the original Priory Church was incorporated into the post-Reformation parish church. Anyone with an eye for ecclesiastical architecture will find this a rewarding stop. There is a magnificent 16th-century painted ceiling, stained glass and restored ruins to see. Boxgrove is also the site of the 1993 excavations that revealed the earliest recorded human habitation in Britain, with bone fragments of Boxgrove man being dated at nearly half-a-million years old. The priory is open every day throughout the year from 0730 until dusk and there is a gift shop. Admission free. Telephone the Tourist Information Centre at Chichester for further details (01243) 775888.

C Tangmere Museum of Military Aviation,
Tangmere Airfield, near Chichester

Tangmere was a front line airfield during the Battle of Britain, when Hitler tried to wipe out the British air force and bomb Britain into submission prior to invading across the Channel. Many of the aerial battles were fought over Sussex as the RAF tried to stop the German Luftwaffe bombing London. Tangmere Museum chronicles this struggle as part of the history of military flying, and the museum contains replica Hurricane and Spitfire fighters of Battle of Britain vintage, along with later fighter aircraft used by the RAF. Open daily from March to October 1000-1730 and in November and February 1000-1630. Charge. Telephone (01243) 775223 for further details.

Goodwood House and Country Park

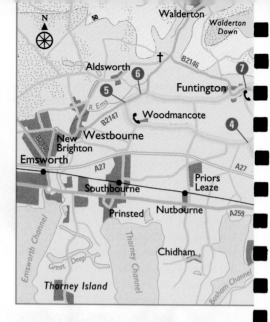

Food and drink

Chichester is well provided with shops, tearooms and restaurants, and there are some well-recommended pubs on the ride.

Bull's Head, Fishbourne

A large pub with a garden, a good range of local and guest beers, children's area and a garden. Food is served at lunchtime and in the evening, with the menu heavy on fish.

Earl of March, Lavant

This pub on the A286 makes a good stop some 16km (10 miles) into the ride. This pub serves good-value food for lunch and evening meals, and the garden gives splendid views of the South Downs. Beers include North Yorkshire's famous Theakston's Best Bitter.

Hogshead, South Street, Chichester

Close to the station – reputed for its moderately-priced food and its immodest selection of 11 real ales.

Mosaic flooring at Fishbourne Palace

Route description

Leave Fishbourne station, TL.

1 XR before the A27, TL.

2 Join B2146.

3 After passing road to Ratham Mill on the left, take next left, passing over stream.

4 Arrive TJ and TL towards Woodmancote.
4km (2.5 miles)

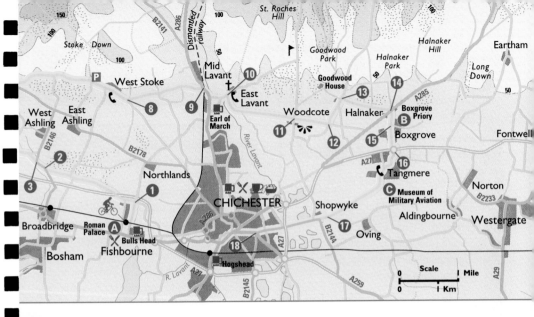

5 Arrive at a TJ with the B2147 and TR.

6 Follow B2147 around right-hand bend, and bear right to go through Funtington.

8km (5 miles)

7 Take LHF off B2147 – at 13km (8 miles) optional stop at a nature trail on the left – continue through West Stoke.

8 Road forks, TL Lavant.

9 TJ with A286 at Mid-Lavant TR then TL to East Lavant. *16km (10 miles)*

10 TR opposite the church in East Lavant.

11 Arrive at the Woodcote XR, SO.

12 Turn left at XR towards East Dean.

13 TR opposite the entrance to Goodwood House. *20km (12.5 miles)*

14 Arrive at the A285 at Halnaker, cross this busy road with care, onto the road to Boxgrove, which leads to the right.

15 Arrive Boxgrove, the Priory is on your left.

16 SO at roundabout at A27. Cross with care – this is a busy junction. This leads through Tangmere village and you pass the museum on your left as you leave the village.

17 Arrive at the hamlet of Shopwyke, join the B2144 and carry straight on. Cross the A27 Chichester by-pass with caution.

18 Join the A259 briefly – this leads to the A286 city centre ring-road – TL then follow SP to the station, where the route finishes.

28.5km (17.5 miles)

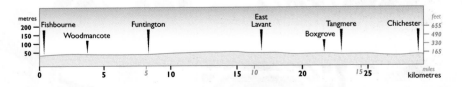

BATTLE OF HASTINGS LOOP – A TOUR OF 1066 COUNTRY

Route information

Distance   29.5km (18.5 miles)

Grade   Moderate

Terrain   Suitable for moderately fit adults and teenagers. Bikes need low gears (like all-terrain bikes) to climb some hills.

Time to allow   2 hours for this undulating ride.

Getting there by car   Battle is on the A2100, with pay parking in the town.

Getting there by train   The ride starts at Battle Station, on the Tonbridge to Hastings line. Telephone (0345) 484950 for timetable information.

This ride takes you from Battle to Brightling and Darwell Reservoir, returning to Battle. The Battle of Hastings was a turning point in British history. After William the Conqueror landed at Hastings he was met inland at the site now called Battle. The defending forces, tired after a long march, were routed and the King killed. The route passes the site of the 1066 battle. To commemorate his victory, William built an abbey at the site of the battle, and the small town of Battle grew up around it.

Places of interest along the route

A Battle of Hastings site, Battle

This is where the last successful invasion of Britain gained its bridgehead, when William the Conqueror led the Norman conquest in 1066. Battle Abbey stands on the site, built by William in celebration of his victory over King Harold and as penance for the loss of life suffered in the battle. You can see the spot where Harold fell and there is an audio-visual presentation, an exhibition and restored Ice House. The site is open in summer 1000-1800 and from October to April 1000-1600. Charge. Telephone (01424) 773792 for further information.

B Brightling

The village is well worth a visit, proving that all the Norman invasions in the world cannot kill off the eccentric Briton. Brightling was the home of Mad Jack Fuller, a 19th-century local landowner and MP who was rumoured to have spent £50,000 bribing electors. Once elected, he started massive local construction projects including walls and follies to keep the local people occupied. Brightling Churchyard is not easily confused with Cairo, but it does have a pyramid as a mausoleum for Mad Jack Fuller. Brightling Church is dedicated to St Thomas à Becket whose feast day is celebrated on 7 July each year by a wake feast.

ⓒ Battle

The town of Battle is a rewarding end to the ride. Visit the medieval Almonry where you can see a model of the town and stroll around award-winning gardens. Open Monday-Saturday 1000-1630. Telephone (01424) 772727. Buckleys Yesterdays World contains over 30 nostalgic shop and room displays dating from between 1850 and 1950, all containing authentic exhibits. Open every day throughout the year, 1000-1800. Telephone (01424) 775378. Battle Museum of Local History contains displays of local artefacts ranging from a replica of the Bayeux Tapestry to dinosaur remains. Open from April to September 1030-1630 (1400-1700 on Sundays). Charge, but children accompanied by an adult free. Telephone (01424) 775955.

Food and drink

Bayeux Cottage Tearooms, Mount Street, Battle

These tearooms are open from Tuesday to Saturday 1000-1700, Sunday 1030-1700 and closed all day on Monday.

🍺 King's Head, Mount Street, Battle

This pub rewards a summer visit for the flowers alone. The King's Head is a low-beamed pub that dates from the 1400s and boasts open fires, a beer garden and meals at lunchtimes and in the evenings.

🍺 1066, High Street, Battle

Just in case you forgot the local significant date. This pub is close to the Abbey and station, is a regular live music venue and serves food at lunchtimes and in the evenings.

🍺 Fullers Inn, Brightling

Named after the local and (reputedly) mad MP and landowner.

Battle

Route description

Leave Battle station, turn right into the High Street (A2100).

1 Turn off A2100 towards Catsfield, passing site of the Battle of Hastings on your right.

2 Turn left on apex of right-handed bend to Telham Hill.

3 SP Crowhurst TR – short, steep climb out of Crowhurst, keeping to the right as you exit the village.

4 At Henley's Down keep right towards Catsfield.

5 Arrive Catsfield, bear left to TJ with B2204, TL briefly onto main road, then TR.

6km (3.5 miles)

6 Arrive TJ, TR. *9.5km (6 miles)*

7 At the A271 TR in direction of Steven's Crouch.

11km (7 miles)

8 TL to Penhurst on a windy, tree-lined road with a sharp descent before Penhurst.

9 TR at Penhurst, past the church on your right. *15.5km (9.5 miles)*

10 Reach XR with B2096, SO.

16km (10 miles)

11 Arrive Twelve Oaks, take RHF or TL to visit Brightling.

12 TR at Hollingrove to Darwell Reservoir.

13 Arrive Mountfield, TJ, TR.

22.5km (14 miles)

14 Arrive Netherfield, SP Battle, TL at TJ.

15 TR onto A2100 at Battle, note windmill on the left of the main road.

29.5km (18.5 miles)

Battle Abbey

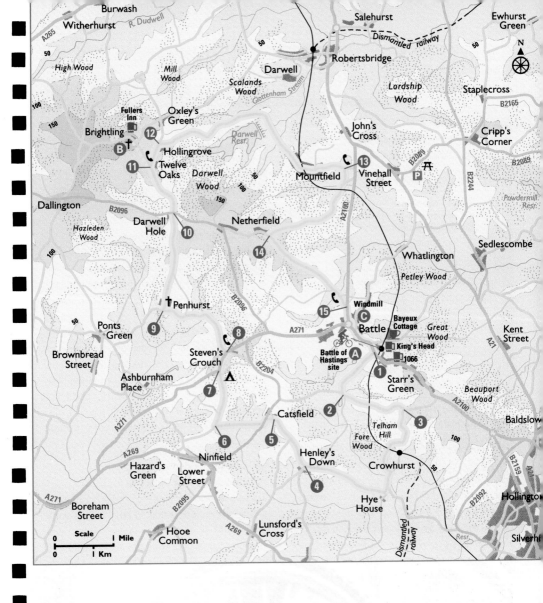

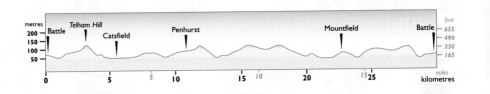

PLAISTOW LOOP – SUSSEX WINE AND CRAFTS

Route information

Distance 30.5km (19 miles)

Grade Moderate

Terrain Undulating, well-surfaced tarmac roads, some long climbs. Suitable for all types of bicycle.

Time to allow 2-4 hours, depending on your fitness.

Getting there by car From Godalming A281 then B2133 through Loxwood, then first right through Ifold to Plaistow where there is off-road parking.

Getting there by train There is no practical railway access to this ride.

The Plaistow loop is a fine introduction to the quiet lanes of Surrey and Sussex. The lanes run through the undulating land between the Surrey Hills and South Downs passing through peaceful villages and offering excellent views over Sussex and the South Downs. The landscape alternates between farmed land and open woodland, and the quiet lanes are dotted with beautiful old houses. The locals are obviously used to an honest rural life – you'll find roadside displays of home laid eggs with an honesty box for contributions, and the lanes between Lurgashall and Plaistow are so full of

pheasants that they almost constitute a road safety hazard.

Places of interest along the route

Ⓐ Kirdford Trug Basket Centre, Kirdford, near Billingshurst

Trug baskets are a Sussex speciality – an old craft dating from probably over three hundred years ago. The baskets are made from sweet chestnut and white willow in the traditional manner, all waste wood from the preparation being used as fuel for the fire that powers the steamer (used to shape the wood). Open Tuesday-Saturday 1000-1800, although the proprietor says that he will always open for a passing cyclist if the closed sign is up. Telephone (01403) 820458 for further information.

Ⓑ Lurgashall Winery, Windfallwood, near Petworth

Sussex is one of England's wine producing areas and the Lurgashall Winery sells a wide range of fruit and flower wines, meads and liqueurs. Samples of wine are available for you to try before you buy and a self-guided winery tour can be made at weekends. The shop also sells tea, coffee and flapjacks as well items such as cider, honey, mustard and fudge. Open every day throughout the year (except for Christmas Day, Boxing Day and New Year's Day) Monday-Saturday 0900-1700 and Sunday 1100-1700. Telephone (01428) 707292.

Food and drink

The bar of Shillinglee Golf Course is open to the public.

Sun Inn, Plaistow
A cyclist-friendly pub with good beer, open fires and bar meals that come with local approval. Lunches Tuesday to Saturday and evening meals Thursday, Friday and Saturday.

Clements Vegetarian Restaurant, Plaistow
Open Tuesday-Saturday 1900-2300. Telephone (01403) 871246 to book.

Plaistow Village Stores, Plaistow
Take the road that runs between the Sun Inn and Holy Trinity Church, 137m (150 yards) on your left. The shop is open Monday-Saturday 0700-2000 and Sunday 1000-1230.

Noah's Ark Pub, Lurgashall
CAMRA-approved. Bar food is served 1200-1400 every day, and 1900-2130 Monday-Saturday.

Lurgashall Shop, Lurgashall
The shop is open Monday-Friday 0900-1800, Saturday 0900-1600 and Sunday 0930-1200.

Lurgashall

Route description

Start at the Sun Inn, Plaistow, following the signpost for Kirdford.

1 Pass the Kirdford Trug Basket Centre.

2 Reach TJ, TR following SP Petworth.
5km (3 miles)

3 SP Northchapel, TR.

4 Arrive TJ, TL following SP Ebernoe, Petworth and Balls Cross.

5 SP Ebernoe, TR.

6 TJ with A283 TR. This is a short, unavoidable stretch of main road.
12.5km (8 miles)

7 TL at SP Lurgashall Winery.

8 Arrive in Lurgashall, Noah's Ark pub to the right, Lurgashall Shop to the left of the village green. To leave the village ride past the pub, SP Haslemere TR. **16km (10 miles)**

9 Arrive TJ, SP Haslemere and Lurgashall Winery, TR and ride to Lurgashall Winery on the left. Leave the Winery, TL, be ready for a steady climb towards Fisherstreet.

10 Arrive TJ, SP to Petworth, Northchapel and Chiddingfold, TR. **21.5km (13.5 miles)**

11 Arrive XR, SP Plaistow 4 miles, SO. Excellent views over the South Downs to the right of this road.

Country lane in Sussex

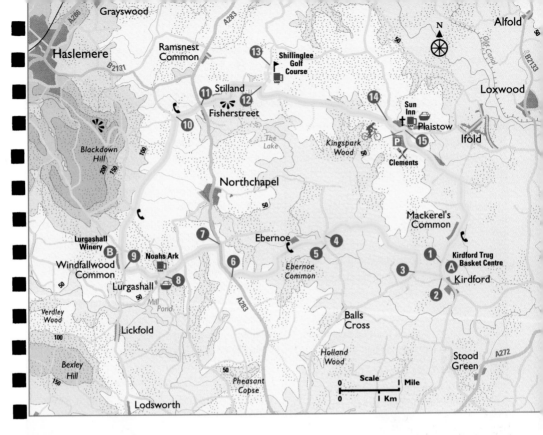

12 SP left Shillinglee Golf Course. The bar is open to the public, serves good lunchtime food and has a pitch and putt course. Even if you don't want to eat or pitch or putt, it's worth diverting down here just for the architecture.

24.5km (15 miles)

13 Rejoin the road from the golf course, TL.

14 TJ, SP Plaistow, TR.

15 Finish ride at the Sun Inn, Plaistow. Ravenous vegetarians could cycle to Clement's Vegetarian Restaurant for a treat.

30.5km (19 miles)

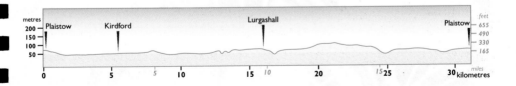

ASHDOWN FOREST AND THE BLUEBELL RAILWAY

Route information

Distance 32km (20 miles)

Grade Moderate

Terrain Tree-lined lanes and quiet roads through open heath. Good surfaces throughout with some hills to tackle. Suitable for most bikes equipped with low gears for hill climbing.

Time to allow 2 hours if you are fit, up to 3 if you dawdle.

Getting there by car The main route starts from the Bluebell Railway's station at Horsted Keynes. Take the A275 from Lewes, left at Danehill to Horsted Keynes, follow signs to Horsted Keynes Station, where there is car parking. A22 from East Grinstead, at Wych Cross join A275, after 5km (3 miles) turn right at Danehill to Horsted Keynes, then follow signs to station.

Getting there by train The route map shows an alternative start from the nearest main line station, East Grinstead, served by Connex South Central. Telephone (0345) 484950 for information.

An undulating loop from Horsted Keynes through the Ashdown Forest villages of Nutley, Splaynes Green and Sheffield Green. Ashdown Forest lanes run through the ridges of the low Weald, an area of ridged, eroded land that lies between the North and South Downs. The Weald used to be extensively covered in forest which survived until the Sussex iron industry flourished in the 16th and 17th centuries, and vast acreages of forest were felled to fuel the furnaces and foundries. One product of the Sussex iron industry was cannon for warships. English ships were reported to have been attacked by Spanish ships, armed from Sussex foundries. The cleared areas became scrub-covered heath, and there have been recent initiatives to reforest the heath to further extend the forest. The heath, while it exists, gives excellent views over this distinctive landscape.

Places of interest along the route

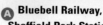 **Bluebell Railway,**
Sheffield Park Station, near Uckfield

The Bluebell Railway runs vintage steam trains between the ride's start at Horsted Keynes and Sheffield Park Station. Horsted Keynes Station is described as the finest preserved station in the country and it is here that the Bluebell Railway restores and maintains its carriages. Special events are held throughout the year. Trains run every weekend, daily from May to September and during Easter week, half-term and bank holidays (except Christmas). Charge.

Telephone (01825) 723777 for further information or (01825) 722370 for a talking timetable.

B Sheffield Park Museum, Sheffield Park Station, near Uckfield

The museum is located at Sheffield Park Station, the headquarters of the Bluebell Railway, where there is one of the largest collections of steam locomotives in Britain and where the Bluebell Railway maintains and restores the locomotives. The museum contains all the paraphernalia and memorabilia that were once commonplace on train journeys. There is a souvenir shop. Opening times and telephone numbers as for the Bluebell Railway above.

C Ashdown Forest, Sussex

Ashdown Forest is the fictitious Hundred Aker Wood home of Winnie-the-Pooh and Christopher Robin. It covers more than 5261 hectares (13,000 acres), and much of this is open along bridleways (cycling permitted) and footpaths where cycling is forbidden. It is a conservation area, and besides being home to Christopher Robin and friends, you might spot deer in some of the quieter areas reached on this ride.

Food and drink

Both Horsted Keynes and Sheffield Park Stations offer refreshments: Horsted Keynes Station has a Victorian refreshment room; Sheffield Park Station has a bar, offering home-made bar lunches and a self-selection family restaurant.

✕ **Oak Hall Manor Self-Service Restaurant, Sheffield Park Gardens**
off the A275 at direction 21. Telephone for opening times (01825) 790338.

The Bluebell Railway

Route description

To start from East Grinstead Station leave station, TR and after 0.5km (0.3 mile) TR onto the B2110.

1 XR, TR to Weir Wood Reservoir.

2 TL off the B2110, towards Saint Hill and Weir Wood Reservoir. Burial barrows on each side of the track.

3 Arrive and cross reservoir. SO.
4.5km (3 miles)

4 Arrive Tyes Cross, staggered XR, SO.

5 Road forks, take the LHF.

6 Arrive Westlands, TL, joining the main route at point 11. *8.5km (5 miles)*

The main route (note that the accumulated km/miles start at 0 from Horsted Keynes Station):

7 Leave Horsted Keynes Station TL direction Horsted Keynes.

8 TJ TL direction Cinder Hill.

9 TR after 1.5km (1 mile).

10 TR direction Westlands.

11 At 3.5km (2 miles) road forks, RHF.

12 TL at 4km (2.5 miles).

13 TJ TR direction Wych Cross.
5.5km (3.5 miles)

14 XR with A22, go SO. Continue through woodland.

15 Arrive Coleman's Hatch TJ, TR.
11km (7 miles)

16 TR to join B2026.

17 XR following SP to Nutley TR.
16km (10 miles)

18 Arrive at XR and TL into Nutley.

19 Pass the church and TR.
18.5km (11.5 miles)

20 TR as you enter Splaynes Green.

21 Arrive at Sheffield Green XR and go SO.
25km (15.5 miles)

22 Arrive Freshfield Crossways, staggered TJ, SO.

23 Arrive at junction, TR to Horsted Keynes.

24 XR SO towards Horsted Keynes Station.
31km (19 miles)

25. TL to Horsted Keynes Station and the end of the ride or continue to direction 11 and return to East Grinstead Station.
32km (20 miles)

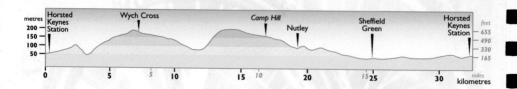

STEDHAM COMMON TO THE FOOT OF THE DOWNS

Route information

Distance 33.5km (21 miles)

Grade Moderate

Terrain Three testing hills and some exhilarating descents. The ride is on-road except for a short section of bridleway. Suitable for touring, hybrid and all-terrain bikes.

Time to allow 2-3 hours.

Getting there by car A325 or A3 onto the B3006 Liss road. Car parking at Liss Station.

Getting there by train South West Trains on the Waterloo to Portsmouth line call at Liss station. Telephone (0345) 484950 for information.

This ride takes you from Liss through country lanes to the villages that lie at the foot of the steep scarp slope of the South Downs. While it does have some hills to tackle, this ride provides an excellent view of the South Downs without having to climb onto the tops. The ride follows the road except for 1km (0.6 mile) of sandy bridleway, but some of the roads are

narrow single track lanes, with gravel at the sides and in the middle of the road, so you should ride these sections with care.

Places of interest along the route

A **Stedham Common, West Sussex**

Stedham Common comprises 115 hectares (285 acres) of heath containing Mesolithic and Bronze Age archaeological sites, including several spectacular tumuli (burial mounds dating from the Bronze Age). The heath was also a thoroughfare for the Roman invaders, who characteristically drove a dead straight road through it. The ancient Britons and Romans have abandoned the heath to tourists and common lizards, and this is one of the few large remaining areas of heath in West Sussex. Heathland is a managed environment, and much of the heath in Britain has been overgrown by scrub or commercial timber plantations. The common is now a protected habitat, managed as a nature reserve.

B **St Andrew's Church, Didling**

St Andrew's Church is a small 13th-century shepherds' church that makes a peaceful picnic stop.

Food and drink

Fitzhall Farm, near Stedham Common
Tea, coffee, home-made cakes and bed and breakfast. This stop comes highly recommended by local cyclists, who suggest a visit in the morning when refreshments are served in the house.

Ship Inn, South Harting
Both bar snacks and substantial restaurant meals served at lunchtimes and in the evenings at this CAMRA-endorsed pub.

White Hart, South Harting
Opposite the Ship, serves bar meals at lunchtimes and in the evenings, with a garden to enjoy in summer.

Wyndham Arms, Rogate
CAMRA's Sussex Pub of the Year 1996, and well worth a stop.

A view of the South Downs

Route description

From Liss Station TL along the B3006, after 91.5m (100 yards) TR at the roundabout, signposted B3006 Rogate. Steady climb out of Liss.

1 Arrive at XR with B2070, SO following SP Rogate. Continue through the woods.

2 Arrive at a junction with a bridleway immediately ahead – straight onto the bridleway. The bridleway surface is sandy with occasional tree roots and rocks, so use low gears and watch where your wheels are going. *6.5km (4 miles)*

3 The bridleway ends, TR onto the single track road. This is a quiet, narrow road, but the surface is sandy and gravelly, so ride in the clear wheel tracks and listen out for cars coming around the tight bends.

4 Arrive TJ, TL and be ready for a steady climb. At the bottom of the dip, look to your left for a sign to an unlikely Sussex residence – Chithurst Buddhist Monastery (not open to the public).

5 Arrive at a staggered XR with signposts to Midhurst and Elsted. TR.

6 Arrive at the A272, SO, following SP Elsted and Harting onto Elsted Road. This road runs through the middle of Stedham Common. *11km (7 miles)*

7 The road bears to the right. Fitzhall Farm to the left here.

8 SP Didling 2 miles, TL. From here you can see the scarp slope of the South Downs proper. Don't worry – this ride doesn't need you to climb it.

9 Arrive TJ and TR following SP for Treyford, Harting and Didling Church. Take a diversion to the left to see St. Andrew's Church. *16km (10 miles)*

10 SP Elsted and Harting TL. This road runs parallel to the foot of the Downs – notice how the hill to your left has a scalloped outline, caused by erosion over many thousands of years.

11 Reach TJ in Elsted, TL SP Harting and Petersfield. *19km (12 miles)*

12 XR, SO to enter South Harting.

Cycling in West Sussex

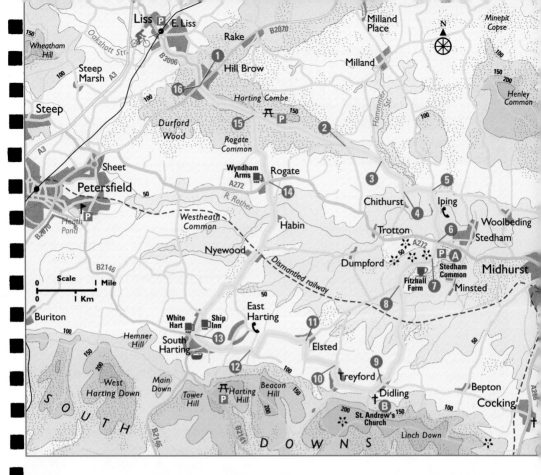

13 TR just after the post box, following SP Rogate and Nyewood. Be ready for a climb out of South Harting, then a fast descent into Nyewood crossing the River Rother at Habin, then a further climb out of Habin.

25.5km (16 miles)

14 Reach XR with A272, SO.

15 SP Hill Brow, Liss and Liphook, TL.

16 XR with B2070, SO onto the B3006 for a fast descent into Liss. TL at the roundabout, to return to the station. *33.5km (21 miles)*

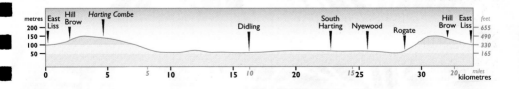

LEWES TO EASTBOURNE ON THE SOUTH DOWNS WAY

Route information

Distance 35.5km (22 miles)

Grade Strenuous

Terrain The ride is 75 per cent off-road on the South Downs Way (SDW), a track with a varied surface (usually bumpy), and which may be strewn with roots, rocks and gravel. Although this sounds daunting, it is tremendous riding with stunning views inland and over the English Channel. This ride is suitable only for all-terrain bicycles and robust hybrid bicycles.

Time to allow 2-3 hours since off-road riding is slower than rolling along road.

Getting there by car Lewes is reached by the A26, A27 and A275, with pay parking in the town.

Getting there by train Lewes Station can be reached from Eastbourne, Brighton and lines that run to Redhill, Surrey. The service is by Connex South Central, and bicycles are carried free. If you use the train, remember that bicycle carriage is at the guard's discretion. Since this is a linear ride you finish away from your car, but trains from Eastbourne to Lewes run up to four times an hour. Telephone (0345) 484950 for information.

This ride takes you from Lewes to the official end of the SDW, where it stops being spectacular chalk downland and becomes urban Britain once again. Eastbourne is a better than average example of urban Britain, with elegant seafront and town centre buildings that have been sensitively developed rather than ravaged, as is common in many coastal resorts. Lewes, at the ride's start, has a lot of history for its size: the site of a bloody Civil War battle; and where Bloody Mary had Protestant dissenters burned at the stake. Tom Paine, a republican revolutionary hailed from Lewes, as did Gideon Mantell, famous for his 19th-century discovery of the fossil dinosaur Iguanadon, and equally famous for reconstructing the skeleton with its thumb misplaced on its snout!

Places of interest along the route

A Lewes Museum of Sussex Archaeology, 169 High Street, Lewes
A vivid display of Sussex archaeology and exhibitions illustrating the importance of Sussex to the history of England. Open Tuesday-Saturday. Telephone (01903) 715149.

B Alfriston
The village is quite beautiful and is well worth a visit to see the close-packed thatched cottages in their traditional village setting. Alfriston Clergy House, a thatched 14th-century Wealden Hall House (see Route 3 for details) is situated in the village and there are plenty of teashops to help quench a cyclist's thirst. Telephone the Boship Tourist Information

Centre on (01323) 442667 for further information on the village.

ⓒ The Long Man of Wilmington, on the SDW, east of Alfriston

The Long Man is a giant figure cut into the hillside. Until the 19th century, the Long Man was only visible in certain light conditions and after a fall of snow, but in 1874 the Long Man was marked out in yellow bricks. During World War II the figure was painted green to prevent enemy aircraft using it as a landmark. In 1969 the original bricks were replaced with concrete blocks and they are regularly painted in white to keep the Long Man visible from a distance. There are several theories as to the figure's origin: fertility symbol; ancient warrior; 18th-century folly. However, lack of historical evidence leaves this open to interpretation. The site of the Long Man is owned by the Sussex Archaeological Society. Telephone them on (01273) 486260 for further information.

ⓓ The Butterfly Centre, Royal Parade, Eastbourne

The lush, tropical rainforest re-created in these glasshouse gardens contains live, free-flying butterflies. You can see all stages of the butterflies' metamorphosis, from the eggs to the mature butterflies, in their natural habitat. Many exotic plants, a lake and a waterfall feature in the gardens. There is a gift shop and coffee shop. Open daily from March to October 1000-1700. Charge. Telephone (01323) 645522.

Food and drink

Gardeners Arms, Cliffe High Street, Lewes
Lunchtime meals, real cider and eight real ales available at this CAMRA-recommended pub.

Brewers Arms, High Street, Lewes
Children's room and lunchtime food.

Market Cross, Waterloo Square, Alfriston
A supposedly haunted pub, although the ghosts detract neither from the atmosphere nor the lunches and evening meals.

Eight Bells, High Street, Jevington
A quiet pub with a beer garden, lunchtime and evening food.

Hogshead, South Street, Eastbourne
A CAMRA-listed pub opposite the station and close to the ride's end. Serves lunchtime food.

The Lamb, High Street, Eastbourne
On the A259, this pub is near a 13th-century church and offers lunchtime and evening meals, a garden and a choice of real ale. Children are welcome at lunchtimes.

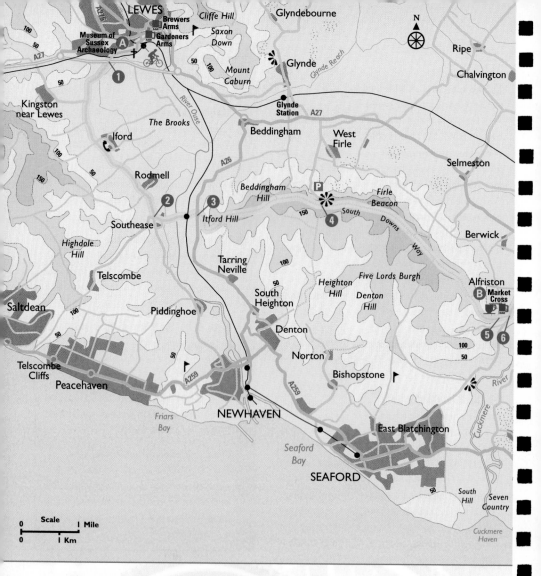

Route description

Leave Lewes Station, TL past the church on your left and the Archaeology Museum on your right, then TL following SP Newhaven.

1 Cross the A27, SO to Rodmell.

2 Arrive Southease XR and TL onto the lane that leads across the River Ouse, across a level crossing. **6.5km (4 miles)**

3 TR onto A26 very briefly, then TL onto the SDW, which is well waymarked with finger posts. Remember that when you are cycling along the SDW, you must give way to walkers and horseriders.

4 Continue along the track, passing a car park and a lane leading to West Firle. **10.5km (6.5 miles)**

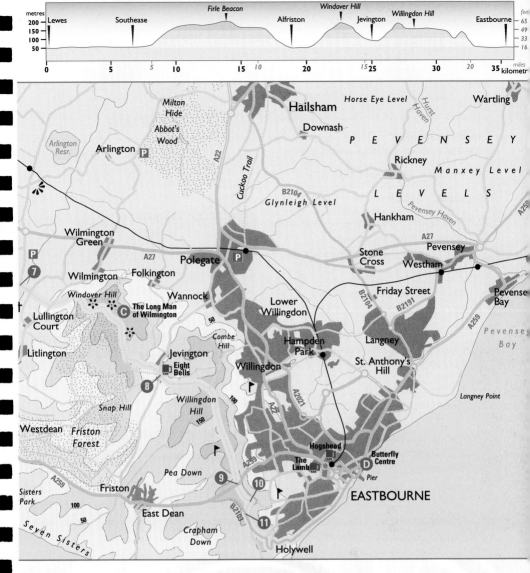

5 Arrive Alfriston and continue through the village. **_17km (10.5 miles)_**

6 TJ, TL and follow finger posts to SDW.

7 TR onto SDW, then arrive at Long Man of Wilmington. **_18km (11 miles)_**

8 SDW arrives at Jevington. The Eight Bells pub is here for refreshment, or SO to continue the SDW. **_23km (14.5 miles)_**

9 SDW crosses the A259, SO.

10 SDW ends, with a final steep descent along a tree-lined track bearing right – easy to miss!

11 TL onto the B2103 and ride along the seafront into Eastbourne to finish. Refresh and relax by visiting the Butterfly Centre.

35.5km (22 miles)

Route 13
BEXLEY HILL AND WEST SUSSEX VILLAGES

Route information

 Distance 39.5km (24.5 miles)

 Grade Strenuous

Terrain The ride is on back lanes and single track roads with one stretch of bridleway, but there are three steep climbs.

 Time to allow 2-3 hours if riding all the way, 3-4 hours if you walk the hills.

 Getting there by car A325 or A3 onto the B3006 Liss road. Car parking at Liss Station.

Getting there by train South West Trains on the Waterloo-Portsmouth line call at Liss Station. Telephone (0345) 484950 for timetable information.

This ride runs from Liss on the edge of the Downs into the rolling countryside to the east of the valley between the South Downs and the Surrey Hills. Sussex is a hilly county, and three of the hills on this ride are steep, meriting its strenuous rating. If you're not too proud to walk the hilliest sections, this will make a pleasant long afternoon ride. This route was planned around finding attractive, quiet back roads, and many of the roads narrow down to gravelly single track lanes with passing places. Many of the buildings on the route have jaundice-yellow woodwork – this is feudal England in the 20th

century, as all the properties sporting this garish decor belong to the Cowdray Estate. Signs on the route warn the unwary about adders – watch where you step if you go for a walk.

Places of interest along the route

Ⓐ Hollycombe Steam Collection, Iron Hill, Liphook

One mile off the marked route. Hollycombe is one of Britain's most comprehensive collections of steam-driven machinery, with reputedly the largest steam fairground in the country. Run by volunteers, the site also includes a woodland garden, a café serving light refreshments and a gift shop. Open daily from Good Friday to mid-October 1300-1800, with rides starting at 1400. Charge. Telephone (01428) 724900.

Ⓑ Lurgashall Winery, Windfallwood, Lurgashall, near Petworth

Sussex is one of England's wine-producing regions, and the Lurgashall Winery boasts a fine range of fruit and flower wines, meads and liqueurs, produced using locally gathered ingredients wherever possible. The winery is located in converted 17th and 19th-century farm buildings and has won three awards for the restoration work. Self-guided winery tours can be made at weekends and there is also a medieval herb garden to visit. You can sample the wine in the Winery Shop before you buy. The shop also sells cider, honey, mustard, fudge and other gift items. Tea, coffee and flapjacks are available (excellent for a tired, hungry cyclist). Open every day throughout the year (except for

Christmas Day, Boxing Day and New Year's Day) 0900-1700 Monday-Saturday, 1100-1700 on Sundays. Telephone (01428) 707292.

ⓒ The Malt House,
Chithurst, near Rogate

The Malt House gardens are part of the National Garden Scheme and are open to the public on certain days during April and May and at other times for pre-arranged visits. The gardens consist of a 2 hectare (5 acre) garden of flowering shrubs, including exceptional azaleas and rhododendrons, and 20 hectares (50 acres) of woodland walks. For detailed information on when the gardens are open to the public, telephone the National Garden Scheme on (01483) 211535.

Food and drink

Refreshments are available at the Hollycombe Steam Collection and Lurgashall Winery. There are shops in Milland and Fernhurst.

Red Lion, Fernhurst Village Green
To the left of the village green as you leave Church Lane following direction 8. Serves bar meals and real ale.

Lickfold Inn, Lickfold crossroads
Real ale, beer garden and bar meals in this 16th-century public house which has the most striking pub architecture you will ever see.

White Horse, Easebourne
Well-recommended by locals for the quality of both its food and drink. A much-needed stop after Bexley Hill.

The South Downs, West Sussex

Route description

Leave Liss station, TL. At the roundabout take the left hand exit, then right at the signpost Rake 1³/₄ miles.

1 The road forks, take the LHF.

2 TR into St Patrick's Lane – steep climb!

3 At Rake XR, SP Rogate, SO.

4 SP Rake Industries, TL ready for a fast descent.

5 SP Milland, TL. **5.5km (3.5 miles)**

6 Enter Milland, SP Midhurst, SO.

7 SP Fernhurst, TR. Diversion (TL) to Hollycombe Steam Collection here.
11km (7 miles)

8 Arrive at Fernhurst XR (15km/9.5 miles) – there are shops here, should you need a snack. SO into Church Lane and follow the road as it runs to the right of the village green. The Red Lion pub overlooks the village green. Past the green, follow SP for Haslemere, Liphook and Midhurst.

9 Sharp left bend, SP Lodshall, Lurgashall and Lickfold. Start climbing a steep hill, and look to your right for excellent views towards the South Downs. Notice the traditionally laid hedge on your left.

10 Lickfold TJ, TR past Lickfold Inn. TL for Lurgashall Winery. **19km (12 miles)**

11 SP Bexley Hill at fork in the road, TR. Steep climb ahead.

12 White Horse pub on the right comes well recommended by locals. A272, TR, then TR again, SP Fernhurst and Haslemere.
25km (15.5 miles)

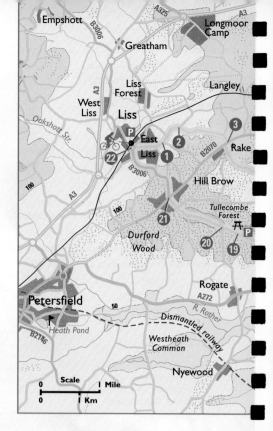

13 Cross the A286, SO following the SP Woolbeding.

14 SP Liphook, Linch and St Cuthman's, TR.

15 SP Stedham TL. This picturesque lane offers excellent views to the south. Keep SO, heading due west across two staggered crossroads. Note optional forest walk and footpath leading to the site of a fort.

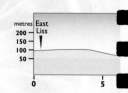

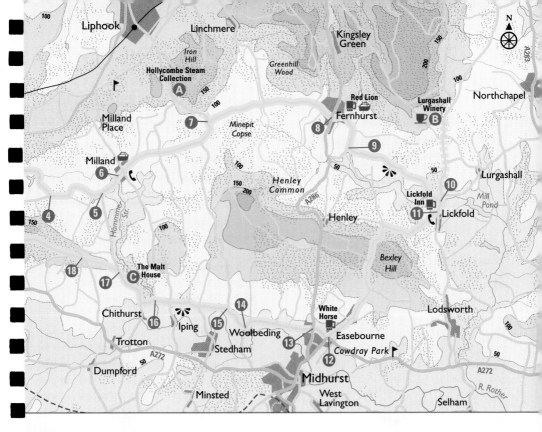

16 Shortly after crossing the stream, look for a sharp TR up a single track road. The Malt House and its beautiful gardens (open to the public during the National Garden Scheme) are here.

31km (19 miles)

17 TL down the bridleway – note the loose surface and ride carefully.

18 XR, SO. Notice the coppicing and warning about adders on your left.

19 Pass Tullecombe Forest Walk and picnic site on your right.

35.5km (22 miles)

20 XR, SO following signposts for Liss 2³/₄ miles.

21 Cross the B2070 onto the B3006.

22 Arrive at Liss roundabout, TL to the station.

39.5km (24.5 miles)

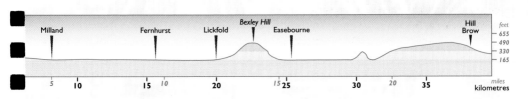

HERSTMONCEUX CASTLE VIA THE CUCKOO TRAIL

Route information

Distance 43km (27 miles)

Grade Moderate

Terrain Suitable for families with teenagers – half of the ride is off-road and the return is on quiet lanes. Most bikes with gears (to cope with some not too taxing hills) will manage this route.

Time to allow 2-4 hours, but the grounds of Herstmonceux Castle alone could divert you for a further 2 hours.

Getting there by car Polegate is on the A27 Pevensey to Brighton road, with car parking at Polegate Station.

Getting there by train Polegate Station is on the Brighton-Eastbourne-Ashford line, run by Connex South Central, which carries bicycles free during off-peak hours. For timetable enquiries telephone (0345) 484950.

From Polegate Station to Heathfield on the Cuckoo Trail, returning to Polegate on rolling back lanes and the Pevensey Levels. The ride is undemanding, with the first 8 miles on the traffic-free Cuckoo Trail, then from Hailsham to Herstmonceux on gently hilly lanes. You will finish on the flat coastal plain of the Pevensey Levels, which are covered with streams and small rivers, draining the hilly Weald into the

sea. Herstmonceux Castle and grounds are beautiful, and this is the site of the former Greenwich Observatory which moved from London to Sussex to escape the growing smog.

Places of interest along the route

A Herstmonceux Castle, Hailsham

Herstmonceux Castle was completed in 1446 and has changed hands several times since then. In 1932 it was bought by the Admiralty as a new home for the Royal Greenwich Observatory. The Observatory left the site in 1993 but there is a Science Centre in its old buildings. All exhibits are designed to be touched and experimented with. The castle grounds are magnificent and include a moat, formal and herb gardens, chestnut avenue, rhododendron garden and woodland walks. The castle itself is not open to the public but the Science Centre and gardens are open daily from April to September 1000-1800. Charge. Telephone (01323) 833816.

B Polegate Windmill, Polegate

Polegate Windmill is situated off the A22, south of Polegate. One of the finest industrial monuments in Sussex, it was built in 1817, in brick with four floors, and restored to working order in 1967. Most of the machinery is the original and there is a museum of milling in the adjoining store room. Visitors can climb the red brick tower and watch the mill sails turn on windy days. Tea and cakes available. Open on Sundays and Bank Holidays from Easter to the end of September, and on Wednesdays in August. Charge. Telephone (01323) 482413.

Food and drink

Hailsham and Polegate have a selection of shops, and refreshments are available at Herstmonceux Castle and Polegate Windmill.

Junction Tavern, Polegate
Close to the Cuckoo Trail start. Real ale, open fires, midday and evening meals, CAMRA-recommended.

The Mill Coffee Shop, Polegate
For snacks and light refreshments.

Golden Martlet, Hellingly
Comfortable pub offering meals at midday and in the evenings. There is a garden and children are welcome.

Grenadier, Hailsham
Serves CAMRA-approved locally brewed beer, including seasonally-brewed specials. Bar meals at lunchtimes only, public bar, lounge and beer garden. Popular with Cuckoo Trail walkers and cyclists.

Old Loom Mill, Hailsham
Tea, coffee, cakes and lunch next to the route.

Woodgate Cottage Tearooms, Vines Cross
Open at weekends from Easter to October 1100-1730.

Brewers Arms, Herstmonceux (on the A271)
Real ales with guest beers and food lunchtimes and evenings except Tuesdays.

Herstmonceux Castle

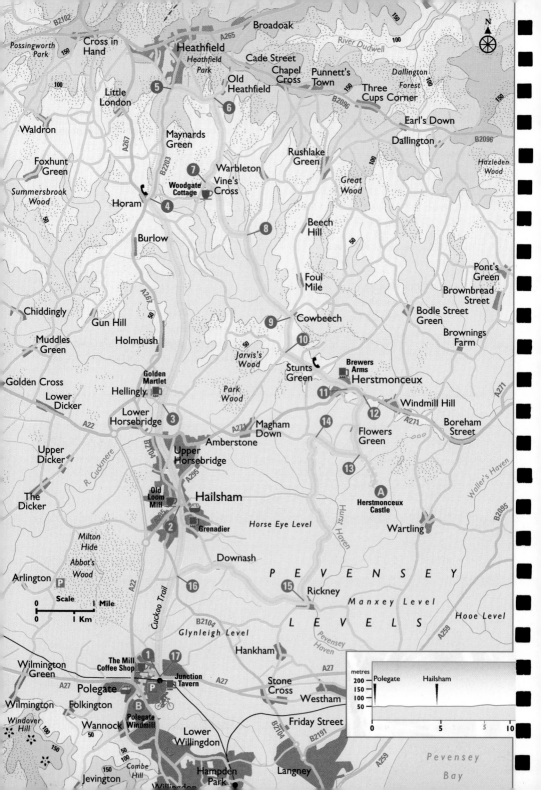

Route description

1 Leave Polegate Station TR. At TJ with A27 TR then first left into School Lane, and the trail entrance is ahead of you as the road bends left.

2 Arrive Hailsham. The trail kinks right into Station Road for a short road link which turns left then sharp right to continue through Hailsham centre, after passing under London Road. The trail joins a further short road link (The Cedars) and leaves Hailsham.

5km (3 miles)

3 The trail passes Hellingly (the Golden Martlet is just off the trail). *8km (5 miles)*

4 Arrive Horam. At the access point (clearly marked) after the short road link, leave the trail for the B2203. TR towards Heathfield.

5 TR towards Old Heathfield.

16km (10 miles)

6 SP Vine's Cross, TR.

7 Arrive at Vine's Cross (Woodgate Cottage Tearooms here). At the TJ, TL.

19.5km (12 miles)

8 Arrive at a TJ, TR.

9 Arrive at Cowbeech TJ, TR.

24.5km (15 miles)

10 Arrive XR, SP Herstmonceux, TL.

25.5km (16 miles)

11 XR, SO onto A271 to Herstmonceux. Pub refreshment here.

12 TR to Flowers Green.

13 After passing through Flowers Green, TR (or SO to Herstmonceux Castle).

29.5km (18.5 miles)

14 TL for a long, flat stretch along Horse Eye Level.

15 Arrive at Rickney TJ and TR.

35.5km (22 miles)

16 Arrive at TJ with B2104, TR and a short distance later rejoin the Cuckoo Trail and TL towards Polegate.

17 Arrive at the end of the Cuckoo Trail in Polegate. Refreshments at the Junction Tavern and a chance to see Polegate Windmill.

43km (27 miles)

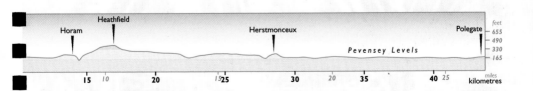

SELBORNE'S NATURAL HISTORY AND THE MEON VALLEY

Route information

Distance 57km (35.5 miles)

Grade Moderate

Terrain Well-surfaced country lanes with occasional stretches of gravel-strewn single track road. Some long hills, and one steep climb after Selborne. Suitable for road bikes, hybrids and all-terrain bikes with road tyres fitted.

Time to allow 3-5 hours, but there is the potential for a long stop in Selborne.

Getting there by car Reach Petersfield on the A3 London to Portsmouth road, turn onto the A272 which has signs to the station for pay and display car parking.

Getting there by train Petersfield is well served by South West Trains on the Waterloo to Portsmouth Line. Telephone (0345) 484950 for information.

From Petersfield station on the edge of the South Downs, running into the Meon Valley, through Selborne and returning to Petersfield. The Meon Valley is a beautiful westerly extension to the South Downs. East Meon is a most beautiful village, with well-preserved close-timbered houses, which are typical of this area's architecture. The lanes around here *are peaceful, and when you cross the busy A roads, prepare to be shocked at the volume of traffic compared to the near-deserted back roads you are riding.*

Places of interest along the route

Ⓐ East Meon
The village of East Meon is a beautiful, well-preserved village that suffers from tourists on summer weekends. Well worth a visit; turn left off the route in East Meon.

Ⓑ Selborne, near Alton
The attractive village of Selborne is a naturalist's delight: nature reserve, Site of Special Scientific Interest, and home to Gilbert White, the famous 18th-century naturalist who immortalised the village in his book *The Natural History of Selborne*. There is a gallery of foot and mouth painting artists and a craft centre in the village.

Ⓒ The Wakes, Selborne, near Alton
The Wakes is an 18th-century country house, home to Gilbert White for most of his life. The garden, well-documented through White's writing, is in the process of restoration but is already well worth a visit. Also at The Wakes is a museum dedicated to Frank Oates, who explored South America and South Africa, and Captain Lawrence Oates, valiant casualty of the ill-fated Scott expedition to the South Pole in 1912. There is a teashop and gift shop. Open daily from the end of March to Christmas, and at weekends only January to March 1100-1700. Charge. Telephone (01420) 511275.

Food and drink

Refreshments are well-spaced on this ride, so be prepared. Petersfield has a good range of shops and pubs close to the station. Refreshments (based on 18th-century recipes) are available at The Wakes.

The Anchor, Ropley
A friendly pub with real ale, a beer garden and reasonably-priced food.

The George, East Meon
Village pub serving real ale and an excellent choice of food.

Ropley Stores, Ropley
In the village on your right. Open Monday-Friday 0900-1730, Saturday 0900-1200, closed Sunday.

The Queens, Selborne
One of the few British pubs that still has a coveted Cyclists' Touring Club plaque to commend it as a cyclist-friendly pub. Reasonably-priced food, children's garden, no meals on Sunday evening, CAMRA-recommended.

Selborne Arms, Selborne
Real ale and a guaranteed choice of vegetarian food. Good Sunday lunches but no meals on Sunday evening. CAMRA-commended.

East Meon

Route description

Leave the station, TL across the level crossing.

1 At the roundabout SP Steep, take the right exit.

2 XR SO.

3 SP High Cross, TL.   **4.5km (3 miles)**

4 At High Cross, take LHF by Church.

5 Arrive A272 XR, SO.   **9.5km (6 miles)**

6 TJ, SP East Meon, TR, through East Meon.

7 Unmarked right turn, look for Westbury House on your left just before it. At XR with A272, SO.   **16km (10 miles)**

8 TJ TR, then XR, SP Alton 8 miles, TL.
20km (12.5 miles)

9 XR with A32, SP West Tisted, SO. At West Tisted, keep right through the village.

10 TJ, TL to Ropley.   **26km (16 miles)**

11 TR SP Ropley Church, then first TR again. Through Ropley.

12 Take the unmarked left turn. At TJ TR, then immediate TR into Kitwood Lane.

13 TJ TR, then unsigned TL.

14 TJ TR, then road forks, take LHF. At XR with A32, SO SP Selborne.
37.5km (23.5 miles)

15 SP Selborne TL. Through Selborne on B3006.

16 SP Newton Valence, TR.

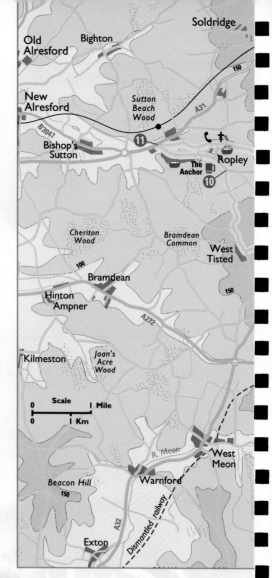

17 SP Hawkley TL.   **45km (28 miles)**

18 SP Steep Marsh, Wheatham, TR. Then follow SP Petersfield.   **50.5km (31.5 miles)**

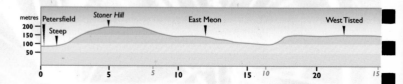

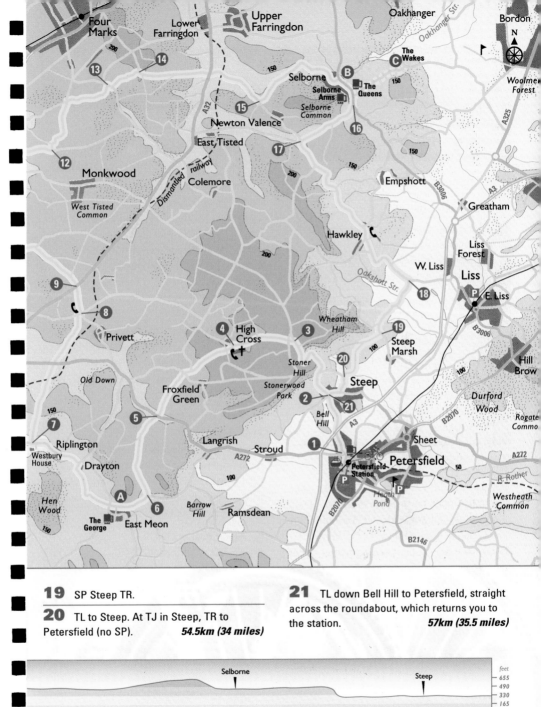

19 SP Steep TR.

20 TL to Steep. At TJ in Steep, TR to Petersfield (no SP). **54.5km (34 miles)**

21 TL down Bell Hill to Petersfield, straight across the roundabout, which returns you to the station. **57km (35.5 miles)**

PETWORTH HOUSE AND THE NORTH WEST WEALD

Route information

Distance   58km (36 miles)

Grade   Strenuous

Terrain   Suitable for the moderately fit of 16 years and up, riding bikes with plenty of gears to cope with the undulating lanes on the route.

Time to allow   Around 4 hours.

Getting there by car   Amberley Station (limited parking nearby) is on the B2139, reached by A29 or A284.

Getting there by train   Amberley Station is on the Connex South Central Line from Littlehampton. Telephone (0345) 484950.

This loop offers all the beauty of the South Downs, without the agony of having to climb the 200m (656 feet) onto the tops. From Amberley in the South Downs the route runs north into the terrain known as the North West Weald and the eroded forest-covered ridges around Petworth and Kirdford, and finishes along the more gentle lanes that` run southwards to the foot of the South Downs at Storrington. The route runs close to the village of Fittleworth, where Edward Elgar lived and composed his cello concerto.

Places of interest along the route

Ⓐ Amberley Museum, Amberley, near Arundel

The village is widely reckoned to be one of the most beautiful in the country, with its 12th-century church and castle (the castle is not open to the public). The museum, next door to the station, features old crafts and industries including the blacksmith and the broom maker. There are steam-driven vehicles, vintage wirelesses and a narrow gauge railway, as well as a nature trail. Open from late March to October, Wednesday-Sunday and Bank Holidays (daily during school holidays) 1000-1700. Charge. Telephone (01798) 831370.

Ⓑ Amberley Wild Brooks, Amberley

A track past Amberley Church leads to the River Arun river meadows, known as Amberley Wild Brooks, a site of interest to ornithologists as the regularly-flooded plains attract flocks of geese and wading birds.

Ⓒ Bignor Roman Villa, Bignor, near Pulborough

This excavated site has many mosaic floors, discovered in 1811 and displayed under cover. One mosaic is the longest on display in the country, at 24.5 metres (80 feet). The museum tells the story of the villa and contains the numerous artefacts discovered on the site. Gift shop and cafeteria. Open March, April, May and October (closed Mondays except Bank Holidays) 1000-1700; daily from June to September 1000-1800. Charge. Telephone (01798) 869259.

ⓓ Petworth House and Park, Petworth

The 600-year-old house contains the National Trust's finest art collection as well as state rooms and restored kitchens. The park was landscaped by Capability Brown and offers two lakes, marvellous views and walks, and a herd of fallow deer. Gift shop. The park is open daily all year 0800 until dusk (28-30 June, closed from 1200). The house is open daily from end March to end October (except Mondays and Fridays, but open Good Friday and Bank Holidays) 1300-1730. Entrance to the park is free but there is a charge for the house. Telephone (01798) 342207.

The Kirdford Trug Basket Centre is near direction 8. See Route 9 for details.

Food and drink

Refreshments are available at Amberley, Bignor Roman Villa and Petworth House.

Bury Stores
3km (2 miles) from the start of the ride.

Tudor Cottage Café, Sadlers Row, Petworth
Open weekdays 0900-1800, Saturdays 0900-1700, Sundays 1000-1800.

Foresters Arms, Kirdford
15th-century pub serving real ale, lunchtime and evening meals (except Tuesdays).

Fishers Farm Park, Wisborough Green
Café open all year round 1000-1700, offering coffee, lunch and tea.

Queen's Head, West Chiltington
A traditional pub with beer garden and open fires. Lunchtime and evening meals.

Petworth House and Park

Route description

Leave Amberley Station, TL along the B2139, then TR SP Bury.

1 Arrive XR at Bury, SO then meet XR with A29, SO for 3.5km (2 miles).

2 TR then SO through West Burton. TL here to visit Bignor Roman Villa – well signed.

3 Arrive at XR, TR following SP to Petworth.
8.5 km (5 miles)

4 Arrive TJ, TL towards Petworth. Then road forks, take RHF.

5 Meet A283 at Petworth. SO through town on A283 – caution, this is a busy road.
13km (8 miles)

6 Exit Petworth on A283, TR SP Kirdford.

7 Bear right to Kirdford. *19.5km (12 miles)*

8 Having ridden through Kirdford, SP Wisborough Green, TL.

9 Arrive at Wisborough Green XR, SO.
25km (15.5 miles)

10 Arrive at the B2133, TR.

11 At TJ with A272, TL onto main road then first left.

12 TJ with the A29 TR for short, unavoidable stretch of main road.
33km (20.5 miles)

13 TL off A29, direction of Barns Green. Note that the road becomes very narrow – ride with care.

14 Arrive at XR, TR. *36.5km (22.5 miles)*

15 Arrive at A272 TL for short stretch of main road. TR SP Chiltington, crossing the B2133.
39km (24 miles)

16 Arrive West Chiltington, TR at the TJ.
45km (28 miles)

17 Arrive West Chiltington Common XR, SO.

18 Road forks, take RHF towards Storrington.
48km (30 miles)

19 Arrive at the A283, TR through Storrington.
50km (31 miles)

20 TL onto B2139 following SP Amberley.

21 Ride ends at Amberley Station.
58km (36 miles)

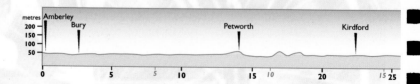

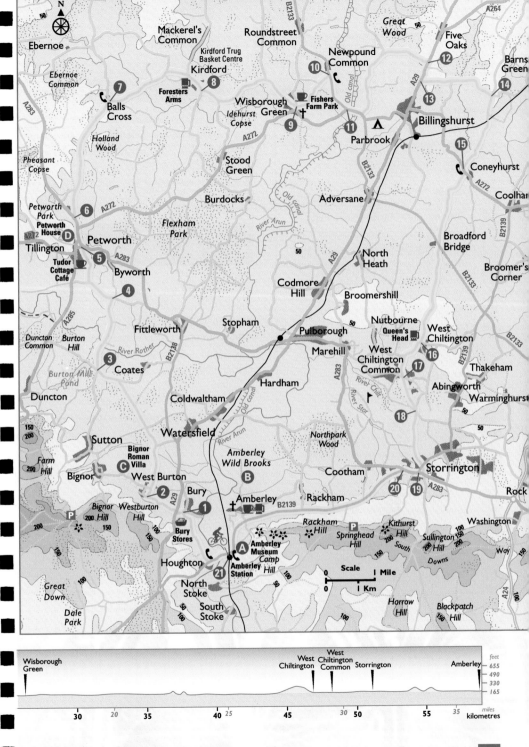

PEVENSEY LEVELS TO BRIGHTLING AND BATTLE

Route information

Distance 59.5km (37 miles)

Grade Strenuous

Terrain Suitable for road bikes, tourers, hybrids and all-terrain bikes fitted with slick, road-going tyres. This quite lengthy ride runs through the flat coastal plain of the Pevensey Levels to the moderately hilly terrain around Brightling and Darwell Reservoir and is suitable for older teenagers and upwards with moderate cycling experience. The roads are all well tarmacked.

Time to allow 3-5 hours.

Getting there by car Pevensey is on the A27 from Brighton and the A259 from Hastings and Bexhill. Pevensey has off-street parking.

Getting there by train Pevensey Bay Station is on the Connex South Central Brighton to Ashford line. Bicycles are carried free off-peak. Telephone (0345) 484950 for enquiries.

This route takes you from Pevensey to Wartling, Brightling, Darwell Reservoir and Battle, returning to Pevensey. Pevensey is the former Roman fort of Anderina. It is an excellent example of the way that the south coastline is silting – William the Conqueror landed his armies at Pevensey, on the coast – now it is more than 2 miles inland. From his beachhead at Pevensey, William fought the English Army at what is now the attractive town of Battle. After some hilly riding around Brightling, the last part of the ride is over the flat Pevensey Levels.

Places of interest along the route

A Brightling
During the 19th century Brightling village was home to Mad Jack Fuller, a local landowner who is reputed to have spent £50,000 bribing electors to get himself voted MP. His massive construction projects of walls and follies were intended to provide work for the local population. Probably his greatest folly was the pyramid built in Brightling churchyard in which he is interred.

B Battle
The town of Battle is a good stop for food, drink and culture. See Route 8 for details.

C Battle of Hastings site, Battle
The site of the last comprehensive invasion of Britain and where William the Conqueror killed King Harold in 1066. Battle Abbey, built by William, is on the battle site, together with audio-visual presentations of the battle and an exhibition. Again, see Route 8 for details.

D Pevensey Castle, Pevensey
Pevensey Castle has a long history of military occupation. The Romans built a fort, named Anderina, on the site which fell into Saxon hands when the Romans left Britain. The Normans constructed Pevensey Castle on the

site after their invasion in 1066. The last time the castle was inhabited with any military intent was during World War II. Open daily from April to the end of September 1000-1800, and from October to the end of March Wednesday-Sunday 1000-1600. Charge. Telephone (01323) 762604 for information.

Food and drink

Refreshments are available in Battle and at Pevensey Castle.

Fullers Inn, Brightling
Named after the local (and reputedly) mad MP. Rumour held that after his death, he was buried sitting upright in his pyramid mausoleum, clutching a glass of port.

Bayeux Cottage Tearooms, Mount Street, Battle
Open Tuesday to Saturday 1000-1700, Sunday 1030-1700 and closed all day on Monday.

King's Head, Mount Street, Battle
This is a low-beamed pub dating from the 1400s. It boasts open fires, a beer garden and meals at lunchtimes and in the evenings.

1066, High Street, Battle
Pub close to the Abbey and station. It is a regular live music venue and serves food at lunchtimes and in the evenings.

The Lamb, Wartling
Located right next to the church, and a splendid example of a village pub. Open fires, children's room, garden and morning and evening meals in both the bar and separate restaurant.

Pevensey Castle

Route description

Leave Pevensey Bay Station, TL onto the A259. TR at the High Street then TL following SP to Wartling, cross A27 bypass.

1 Arrive Wartling XR, TL. *6km (3.5 miles)*

2 Arrive A271 TJ, TL then first right.

3 Arrive at TJ, SP to Bodle Street Green, TL. *9.5km (6 miles)*

4 Arrive Bodle Street Green XR (11km/7 miles), TR then take second right at triangular junction (14.5km/9 miles). Arrive TJ and TL. At XR with B2096 SO. *15.5km (9.5 miles)*

5 The road forks, take RHF signed to Brightling, SO through Brightling to Twelve Oaks.

6 TL at Twelve Oaks then TR at Holling Grove towards Darwell Reservoir. Continue past the reservoir. *20.5km (12.5 miles)*

7 Arrive at Mountfield TJ and TR. *27km (17 miles)*

8 Arrive at TJ, TL following SP to Battle. *30.5km (19 miles)*

9 Join the A2100 at Battle, follow main road through town.

10 TR towards Catsfield. *35km (21.5 miles)*

11 TL to Telham Hill.

12 TR towards Crowhurst – there is a short, steep climb out of Crowhurst.

13 Arrive at Hye House TJ and TR. *41km (25.5 miles)*

14 Enter Henley's Down, TL then take RHF.

15 A269 XR, SO. *45km (28 miles)*

16 Arrive at small XR outside Gotham, TR.

17 Arrive TJ with B2095, TL and follow B2095. *50km (31 miles)*

18 TR following SP to Wartling.

19 TL in Wartling, following SP to Pevensey. *55km (34 miles)*

20 Arrive Pevensey, join A259 and return to the ride's end at the station. *59.5km (37 miles)*

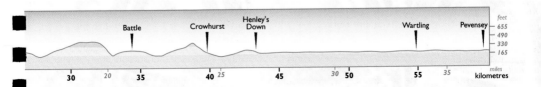

Route 18

WEALD AND DOWNS RIDE TO BRAMBER CASTLE

Route information

Distance 62.5km (39 miles)

Grade Strenuous

Terrain The ride is mainly on quiet lanes and occasional bridleways, but there are some unavoidable short stretches of A and B roads. Climbs are mostly either short and sharp or long and gradual.

Time to allow 4-6 hours.

Getting there by car A24 to Southwater, south of Horsham. Free parking in Church Lane.

Getting there by train Christ's Hospital is served by Connex South Central Trains on the Victoria-Brighton/Portsmouth line. Use the Downs Link (DL) to reach the start of the ride at Southwater – RHF at end of station approach, then TR onto road. TL onto DL just before railway bridge.

This ride wanders southwards through the countryside heading towards the Downs, and the picturesque village of Fulking. From there it runs along the foot of the hills to Bramber and Steyning on the River Adur, before heading back through winding lanes. The landscape of the Weald is generally level, but the valleys of the countless streams which drain its heavy clay soils make for roads which are undulating, to say the least.

Places of interest along the route

Ⓐ Shermanbury Church, near Shermanbury Place

There is no obvious village of Shermanbury, just a scattered parish, and the church is sited next to Shermanbury Place in its private estate. The board outside the church claims it to be 12th-century, but there are signs it may have Saxon origins. The organ loft is odd in being reached by outside stairs. Inside the church, to the right of the door, are some well-worn carvings of heads of early date. Box pews are rare enough but these ones bear the names of the houses and farms whose occupants used them. The church is open only during services, each Sunday morning.

Ⓑ Bramber

Bramber was a thriving port until the River Adur began silting up in the 1300s. The river, then known as Bramber Water, was crossed by a stone bridge with a chapel on the centre pier. Its site is now the car park of the magnificent medieval house, St Mary's, which has been called the finest timber-framed building in Sussex. Built around 1470 as a monastic guest house, it became a private home at the Dissolution and remains one today. Elizabeth I visited the room decorated for her is on display and Charles II sheltered there before escaping to France from Shoreham Harbour. The house and garden are open from Easter to the end of September on Sundays, Thursdays and Bank Holidays 1400-1800. Afternoon teas served in the library. Charge. Telephone (01903) 816205.

C Bramber Castle, Bramber

Built in Norman times, probably to replace an earlier Saxon fort, Bramber's castle was destroyed by Parliamentary forces during the Civil War. A gaunt 'tooth', 23m (76 feet) high, is all that remains of the keep, but you can still see how it guarded the river which once lapped at the foot of its mound. It is now in the care of English Heritage and is open (free of charge) at all reasonable times. Telephone (01732) 778000.

D Knepp Castle

Knepp Castle is just north of Dial Post on the A24. The ruins of the Norman castle stand beside the main road, but the present house is closer to Shipley. It was built in 1809 by John Nash, only to burn down in 1904, and was subsequently rebuilt as an exact replica. In the estate is the 40 hectare (100 acre) Kneppmill Pond, the largest lake in Sussex until the advent of modern reservoirs, and orignally a hammer pond for the ironmaking industry. The estate is not open to the public, but there are rights of way from the Dial Post to Shipley road into the grounds and over the dam of the lake.

E Shipley

As you approach this remote village you are bound to be struck by its enormous church tower. This was no ordinary village church, for it was built in around 1125 by the powerful and wealthy Knights Templars, a military religious order founded by the Crusaders. The other feature of the Shipley skyline is the impressive wooden smock mill. Built in 1879, it was bought in 1906 by the writer Hilaire Belloc. Now fully restored, it is open to the public from Easter to September, on the first and third Sunday of each month 1400-1700. Charge. Telephone (01403) 783188.

Food and drink

There are countless pubs along the route, but some are worth a special mention.

Shepherd and Dog, Fulking
At the west end of the village, this pub can get crowded.

Chequers, High Street, Steyning
Lunchtime and evening meals.

The Fountain, Ashurst
Hilaire Belloc praised the Fountain in his book The Four Men, *written in 1910, and it probably has not changed too much since then.*

George and Dragon, Dragons Green
All that a real country pub should be.

Route description

TR out of the car park at Southwater. At the end of Church Lane TL onto main road and cross bridge over old railway line, now part of the DL.

1 SO at the mini roundabout, then TR into Southwater Street.

2 TR into Reeds Lane, SP Narrow Road, then TL, SP Copsale.

3 TR at TJ, SP Copsale and Maplehurst (6km/4 miles). At Copsale TJ, TL (SP broken).

4 TR at Maplehurst TJ, SP Partidge Green.

5 SO at A272, SP Littleworth and Partidge Green – beware fast traffic. *10.5km (6.5 miles)*

6 Enter Littleworth and SO through village.

7 TJ Partridge Green (end of Littleworth Lane) TL onto B2116, SP Cowfold and Henfield (14.5km/9 miles). TR for village shops. TJ at Shermanbury, TR onto A281, SP Henfield and Albourne. Be careful of traffic.

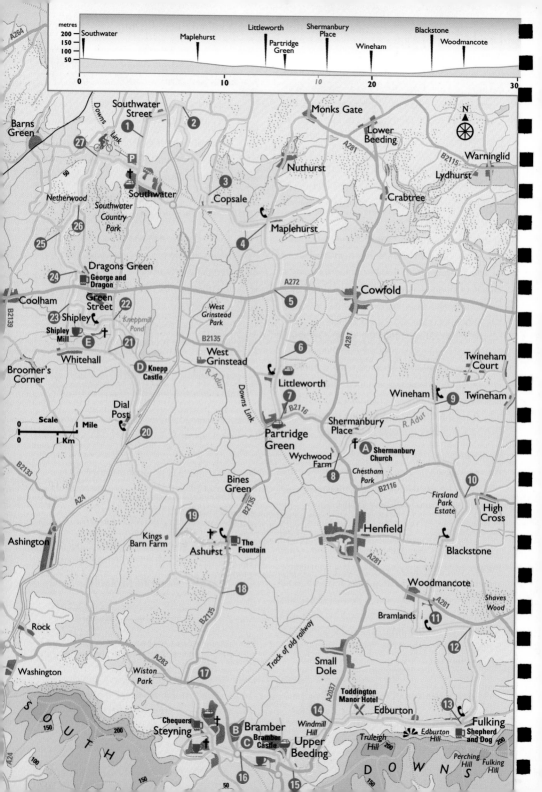

Fulking | Bramber | Steyning | Dial Post | Shipley | Dragons Green | Southwater

20 | 40 | 30 50 | 60

miles
kilometres

8 Watch for SP Bridleway to Shermanbury Parish Church. TL off main road at bend just after Wychwood Farm, though wrought iron gates. SO past Shermanbury Place and church, and onto dirt track. At far end go through gate and onto old lane. TR when it joins tarred driveway. At end of drive, cross cattle grid, then TR onto road.

9 TJ Wineham (no SP), TR and cross river by bridge and arched causeway (20km/12.5 miles). TJ at end of Wineham Lane, TL and rejoin B2116.

10 TR into Blackstone Lane at bend just after Firsland Park Estate (no SP). Continue SO through Blackstone. *24.5km (15 miles)*

11 TJ A281. TR for 100m, then TL into Bramlands Lane, SP Shoreham and Small Dole. After 250m LHF into continuation of Bramlands Lane, SP Caravan Site. Soon after Bramlands, lane bends sharp left.

12 TR at end of Holmbush Lane.
30km (18.5 miles)

13 The lane suddenly emerges at Fulking. Continue along foot of the Downs through Edburton and past Truleigh Manor.

14 Soon after tottington Manor Hotel, TL onto A2037 (35.5km/22 miles). Immediately after Golding Barn petrol station, TR onto unsigned, but obvious byway over Windmill Hill. Caution – chalk surface is slippery when wet. (As alternative, stay on A2037.) Follow byway until it rejoins A2037. (If final length is muddy, leave byway where it passes Maings Farm Road. TL onto road and L again at next TJ to regain A2037.)

15 TR onto A2037. After 300m TR at Rising Sun mini roundabout, SP Upper Beeding. Then, SO next mini roundabout. Through Upper Beeding and over bridge to Bramber.

16 Through Bramber to roundabout by castle. Second exit, Maudlin Lane – steep climb. TR at next TJ. TL at TJ by Steyning approach sign and through town.
40.5km (25 miles)

17 At the A283 TJ,TL then TR, SP B2135 Ashurst and Partidge Green.

18 TL into Spithandle Lane (45.5km/28.5 miles). After 1km, as road bends to left, TR onto bridleway. (Bridleway can be muddy. If ground is wet, continue on B2135 to Ashurst, then TL, SP Church. TL again after 500m, SP Dial Post.)

19 Bridleway joins the road (and alternative route) at sharp bend by entrance to Kings Barn Farm. SO.

20 At A24 staggered XR, SO SP Dial Post (51km/31.5 miles). Take care. At Dial Post LHF into Swallows Lane, SP Shipley.

21 At junction follow road to right, SP Shipley and Southwater.

22 TL at Red Lane, SP Shipley
55km (34 miles)

23 TR at TJ, SP Coolham and Dragons Green, then SO at A272 after 600m.

24 TJ by George and Dragon pub, TL into Bakers Lane, SP Brooks Green.

25 At triangular junction RHF, SP Marlpost and Southwater.

26 TJ TL, SP Southwater and Barns Green.
60km (37.5 miles)

27 TR into Bonfire Hill, SP Southwater. Car park and finish is just beyond church.
62.5km (39 miles)

HOLLYCOMBE TO HASLEMERE ALONG THE FOOT OF THE DOWNS

Route information

Distance 63km (39 miles)

Grade Strenuous

Terrain Like most of Sussex, the terrain is hilly, especially the lanes south and east of Haslemere. This is a ride for the fit, on road or mountain bikes with hill climbing gears and slick road tyres.

Time to allow 3-5 hours.

Getting there by car The A286 from Chichester runs through Haslemere. Turn onto the B2131 to Haslemere Station, where there is pay-and-display parking.

Getting there by train Haslemere is on the South West Trains London Waterloo-Portsmouth main line. Bicycles are carried free in the guard's van. For information telephone (0345) 484950.

This ride – starting at Haslemere on the Hampshire-Sussex border, running to the villages that sit at the foot of the South Downs and returning to Haslemere through quiet Sussex lanes – is an excuse to see some of the most scenic and hilly lanes that Sussex has to offer. It is an area to return to – some of the bridleways at Blackdown (south east of Haslemere) and Hindhead to the north offer excellent opportunities for adventurous

off-road riding. Where breaks in the trees allow, these lanes offer superb views of the South Downs.

Places of interest along the route

Ⓐ Hollycombe Steam Collection, Iron Hill, Liphook

Hollycombe is one of the country's most comprehensive collections of steam-driven machinery and includes a steam fairground. There is also a woodland garden, café and gift shop. Open daily from Good Friday to mid-October 1300-1800, with rides starting at 1400. Charge. Telephone (01428) 724900.

Ⓑ South Harting

This village is reputedly the most westerly in Sussex. It was the home of the novelist Anthony Trollope, author of the *Barchester Chronicles*, and is an attractive place to wander around.

Ⓒ Uppark House, Uppark, South Harting

The National Trust's property has risen like a phoenix from the ashes after the disastrous fire in 1989. The 17th-century house was home to H G Wells when his mother was housekeeper there. The gardens have been restored to their Capability Brown style and there are woodland walks. Restaurant and shop. Open from the end of March to the end of October, Sunday-Thursday. Access to walks 1100-1730, garden open 1200-1730 and house open 1300-1700. Charge. This is a much visited property and booking is advisable. Telephone (01730) 825857 for a recorded message giving information.

Lurgashall Winery, Windfallwood, near Petworth

The winery produces and sells a wide selection of fruit and flower wines, meads and liqueurs and is located in finely restored 17th- and 19th-century farm buildings. Self-guided winery tours can be made at weekends and there is a herb garden to visit. Sample the wines before you buy. Tea, coffee and snacks available. Open every day throughout the year (except Christmas Day, Boxing Day and New Year's Day) Monday-Saturday 0900-1700; Sunday 1100-1700. Telephone (01428) 707292.

Food and drink

Haslemere is well supplied with shops, pubs and cafés. Make sure you have plenty of spare drinks and energy-boosting snacks – the hills make this an energetic ride. Refreshments are available at Hollycombe Steam Collection, Uppark House and Lurgashall Winery.

Wyndham Arms, Rogate
CAMRA's Sussex Pub of the Year 1996, and well worth a stop. Dating from the 1500s, this pub is noted for fine beer and a ghost.

The Ship, South Harting
A low-beamed pub with real ales, and substantial meals and bar snacks served at lunchtimes and in the evenings.

White Hart, South Harting
Opposite the Ship. Serves bar meals at lunchtimes and in the evenings, with a garden to enjoy in summer.

Bluebell Inn, Cocking
Well used to welcoming walkers and cyclists from the South Downs Way. Real ales, a garden and meals available seven days a week, lunchtimes and evenings. Children welcome.

Cocking Post Office and Stores
Shop open Monday-Friday 0600-1800, Saturday 0630-1800, Sunday 0700-1600.

Three Moles, Selham
CAMRA's Pub of the Year 1995, a small, traditional pub – you can quench a thirst here with real ale and cider, but no food is served.

Lickfold Inn, Lickfold crossroads
Sixteenth-century public house – real ale, beer garden, bar meals and the most striking pub architecture.

Route description

Leave the station and turn right along the B2131 following SP for Liphook.

1 As B2131 bears to the right, bear left.

2 Arrive XR, TL through Hollycombe.
5.5km (3.5 miles)

3 TR towards Milland.

4 Arrive at XR, TR following SP Milland.

5 At Milland XR (shops here) SO, until the road forks. Take RHF.
12.5km (8 miles)

6 Arrive at Harting Combe XR, TL.

7 At Rogate Common XR, SO.
15km (9.5 miles)

8 Arrive Rogate. At XR with A272, SO following SP South Harting.
17km (10.5 miles)

9 Enter South Harting. Divert to Uppark House here with a steep climb up the B2146. Otherwise, TL following SP Elsted.
21.5km (13.5 miles)

10 Ride into Elsted. TR following SP Didling, passing through Treyford.
25.5km (16 miles)

11 Arrive Didling, TR following SP to Bepton, SO at Bepton.

12 At Cocking TJ with A286, TL – ride with care, this is a busy road. **33.5km (21 miles)**

13 TR off the A286, and when the road forks take LHF. **34.5km (21.5 miles)**

14 At the XR, SO through Graffham Common towards Selham. **40km (25 miles)**

15 Arrive Selham SO.

16 Arrive at TJ with the A272, TL then TR following SP Lodsworth. Ride through Lodsworth. **43.5km (27 miles)**

17 Pass through Lickfold and shortly afterwards pass Lurgashall Winery.
50km (31 miles)

18 SP Haslemere, TL. **57km (35.5 miles)**

19 Join B2131. TL towards Haslemere.

20 Finish the ride at Haslemere Station.
63km (39 miles)

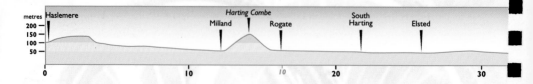

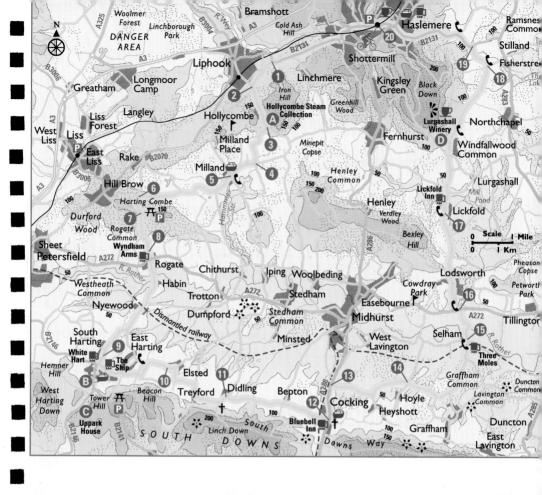

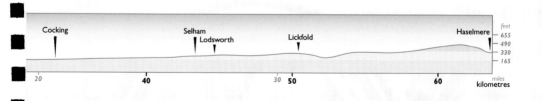

Route information

Distance 65km (40.5 miles)

Grade Strenuous

Terrain The ride starts quite forgivingly on the Pevensey Levels of the Low Weald coastal plain but then runs into the hills and valleys of the southern forest ridge (which account for this ride's strenuous rating). Suitable only for the fit, riding bikes capable of tackling steep hills.

Time to allow 4-6 hours.

Getting there by car Pevensey is on the A27 from Brighton and A259 from Hastings and Bexhill. Pevensey has off-street parking.

Getting there by train Connex South Central stops at Pevensey Bay Station, on the Brighton to Ashford line. Bicycles are carried free off-peak. Enquiries on (0345) 484950.

This ride takes you from the coastal town of Pevensey to Bewl Bridge Reservoir through the Weald villages of Wartling, Burwash and Brightling. Pevensey is the former Roman fort of Anderina and shows quite clearly the way that the British coastline is changing. When William the Conqueror landed at Pevensey in 1066, it was right on the coast, and now silting means that it is more than 2 miles inland. The ride runs through Darwell Wood in the Low Weald, a remnant of the massive forests that used to blanket the entire Weald.

Places of interest along the route

A Pevensey Castle, Pevensey

The castle has a long history of military occupation. Originally the Romans built a fort on the site, which was left to the Saxons when the Romans left Britain. The Normans, after their conquest in 1066, built the castle on the site of the Roman fort, and the castle has periodically been strengthened since. It was last occupied by the military during World War II. Open daily from April to the end of September 1000-1800; and from October to the end of March Wednesday-Sunday 1000-1600. Charge. Telephone (01323) 762604 for information.

B Bateman's, Burwash

Bateman's is a National Trust property, built in 1634 of local sandstone. Between 1902 and 1936 it was home to Rudyard Kipling, author of the *Jungle Book* and *Puck of Pook's Hill*, which was written at Bateman's. You can see Kipling's rooms and mementos of his time in India. The peaceful garden contains a watermill which grinds corn on most Saturdays at 1400. Restaurant and shop. Open from the end of March to the end of October Saturday-Wednesday 1100-1730. Charge. Telephone (01435) 882302.

C Bewl Bridge Reservoir

Southern Water Services constructed the reservoir at Bewl Water between 1973 and

1975. The site covers 486 hectares (1200 acres) and there is a visitors' centre, children's adventure playground and opportunities for walking, cycling, watersports and fishing. Cyclists visiting Bewl Water should keep to the designated tracks and give way to walkers. Refreshments available. Some routes are open all year round but the route around the water is closed during bad weather. The visitors' centre will advise. Free admission. Telephone (01892) 890352/890661.

Ⓓ Brightling

The village of Brightling is well worth a visit – the home of Mad Jack Fuller, landowner and MP of the 19th century, who was rumoured to have spent £50,000 bribing his way into government. Once elected, he started massive local construction projects, including walling his entire estate and building follies, to provide work for the local population. Mad Jack Fuller is buried in the local cemetery – in a large, pyramid-shaped mausoleum, maintaining his mad reputation beyond the grave.

Food and drink

Pevensey has shops for stocking up on food and drink before you leave on this strenuous ride. Pevensey Castle, Bateman's and Bewl Bridge Reservoir all offer opportunities for refreshment.

The Lamb, Wartling
Next door to the church with children's room and garden. Meals served at lunchtimes and in the evenings in both the bar and separate restaurant.

Bell Inn, High Street, Burwash
This has been a CAMRA-praised pub for more than 20 years. Lunchtime and evening meals.

Fullers Inn, Brightling
Named after the local (reputedly) mad MP. Local rumour held that on his death he was buried sitting upright in his pyramid mausoleum, clutching a glass of port.

Pevensey Levels

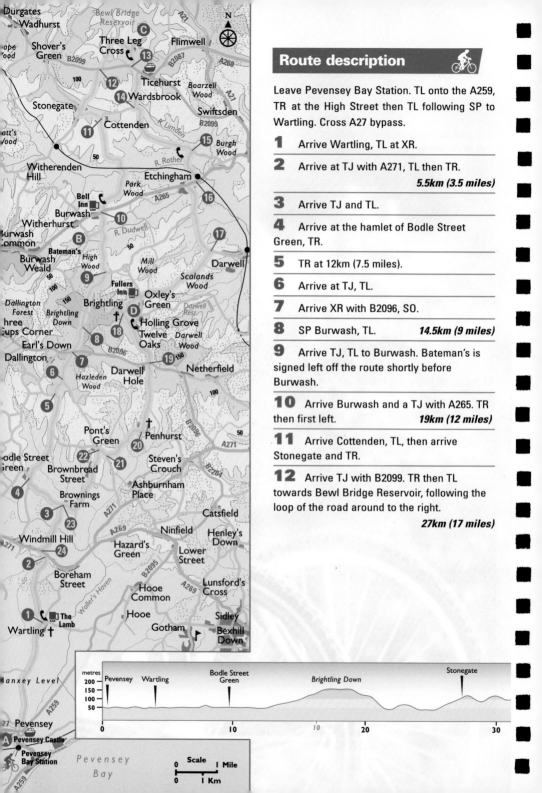

Route description

Leave Pevensey Bay Station. TL onto the A259, TR at the High Street then TL following SP to Wartling. Cross A27 bypass.

1 Arrive Wartling, TL at XR.

2 Arrive at TJ with A271, TL then TR. *5.5km (3.5 miles)*

3 Arrive TJ and TL.

4 Arrive at the hamlet of Bodle Street Green, TR.

5 TR at 12km (7.5 miles).

6 Arrive at TJ, TL.

7 Arrive XR with B2096, SO.

8 SP Burwash, TL. *14.5km (9 miles)*

9 Arrive TJ, TL to Burwash. Bateman's is signed left off the route shortly before Burwash.

10 Arrive Burwash and a TJ with A265. TR then first left. *19km (12 miles)*

11 Arrive Cottenden, TL, then arrive Stonegate and TR.

12 Arrive TJ with B2099. TR then TL towards Bewl Bridge Reservoir, following the loop of the road around to the right. *27km (17 miles)*

13 TJ with B2099, TL into Ticehurst (shops on this road) then TR towards Wardsbrook.

30.5km (19 miles)

14 Arrive TJ and TL.

15 TR to Etchingham Station.

35.5km (22 miles)

16 Arrive A265, TR SP Robertsbridge. TL in the village of Etchingham.

17 SP Brightling, TR. *40km (25 miles)*

18 Arrive Brightling, TL at TJ.

44km (27.5 miles)

19 Arrive at Darwell Hole XR with B2096, SO.

20 Arrive TJ in Penhurst, TR.

49.5km (31 miles)

21 Arrive TJ, TR.

22 TL. If you reach Pont's Green, you've gone too far! This road takes a sharp right before turning left towards A271 and Wartling.

23 TL towards the A271 and Wartling.

55km (34 miles)

24 TJ with A271, TL then TR following SP Wartling. At Wartling, TR following SP Pevensey, finish at the station.

65km (40.5 miles)

Oast houses at Bateman's

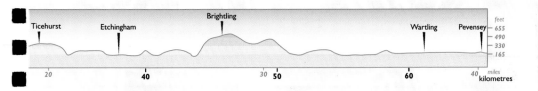

THREE CASTLES LOOP – PEVENSEY, BODIAM AND HERSTMONCEUX

Route information

Distance 65km (40.5 miles)

Grade Moderate

Terrain The ride starts on the flat but by the time the ride leaves the coastal plain at Bexhill, the valleys of the Weald mean that there are regular hills to be climbed. Use a road bike with plenty of low gears, or a mountain bike fitted with high-pressure, road-going tyres.

Time to allow 3-5 hours.

Getting there by car Pevensey is on the A27 from Brighton and A259 from Hastings and Bexhill. Pevensey has off-street parking.

Getting there by train Connex South Central stops at Pevensey Bay Station, on the Brighton to Ashford line. Bicycles are carried free off-peak. Telephone (0345) 484950 for information.

This route starts at Pevensey Castle, riding north inland to Bodiam Castle, then through Brightling and past Herstmonceux Castle, returning to Pevensey. Anyone in doubt of the strategic importance of Sussex throughout history just needs to look at the number of castles scattered around the countryside. Some are proper castles, built for withstanding a determined assault, others are large country homes glorified with battlements.

Places of interest along the route

Ⓐ Pevensey Castle, Pevensey

Once on the shore to defend the coast, Pevensey Castle is now inland due to silting. Originally the site of a Roman fort, Pevensey Castle was the site of William the Conqueror's landing in 1066. The Normans built the castle on the site of the Roman fort. The castle has been periodically strengthened over the centuries and its last military occupation was during World War II. Open daily from April to the end of September 1000-1800; from October to the end of March Wednesday-Sunday 1000-1600. Charge. Telephone (01323) 762604 for information.

Ⓑ Bodiam Castle, Bodiam, Robertsbridge

Bodiam Castle, now owned by the National Trust, looks just as a castle should – sheer walls rising out of a moat. This medieval castle was built in 1385 and is a great place to explore. Although a ruin inside, some of the floors have been replaced. You can climb the spiral staircases, cross the battlements and access the top of the castle where there are wonderful views of the surrounding Sussex countryside. A chapel and great hall add to the atmosphere. There is a small museum which explains the history of the castle and gives an insight into life during medieval times. Lots of space for a picnic. Restaurant and shop. Special events held throughout the year. Charge. Open daily from February to November 1000-1800, or dusk if earlier; from November to January Tuesday-Sunday 1000 to dusk. Closed 24, 25 and 26

December but open New Year's Day. Telephone (01580) 830436.

Ⓒ Herstmonceux Castle, Hailsham

Herstmonceux Castle is another moated castle. It was completed in 1446 and was one of the earliest brick-built buildings of the time. In 1932 it was bought by the Admiralty as a home for the Royal Greenwich Observatory, which moved from London to escape the smog. The Observatory is no longer on the site but there is a Science Centre in its old buildings. The centre contains hands-on exhibits, designed to be touched and experimented with. The castle grounds are magnificent and include a moat, formal and herb gardens, chestnut avenue, rhododendron garden and woodland walks. Tearoom and shop. The castle itself is not open to the public but the Science Centre and gardens are open daily from April to September 1000-1800. Charge. Telephone (01323) 833816.

The site of the Battle of Hastings and the village of Brightling (see Route 8) are also passed on this ride.

Food and drink

Refreshments are available at Pevensey, Bodiam and Herstmonceux Castles.

☕ Bayeux Cottage Tearooms, Mount Street, Battle
Open Tuesday-Saturday 1000-1700, Sunday 1030-1700, closed all day Monday.

🍺 King's Head, Mount Street, Battle
This low-beamed pub dates from the 1400s. Open fires, a beer garden and meals at lunchtimes and in the evenings.

🍺 1066, High Street, Battle
Close to the Abbey and station. Food available at lunchtimes and in the evenings.

🍺 Royal Oak, Whatlington
Few pubs boast a baronial hall and 24.5m- (80 ft-) deep well, but it's only what you expect in this pub dating from the 1400s. Quiet, with open fires and lunchtime and evening food.

🍺 The Ostrich, Robertsbridge
The former Railway Hotel. Beer garden, open fires and bar meals at lunchtimes and in the evenings. Serves a range of locally-brewed real ales.

🍺 Fullers Inn, Brightling
Named after the local (reputedly) mad 19th-century MP.

🍺 The Lamb, Wartling
Next door to the church and a splendid village pub. Children's room, garden, and morning and evening meals in both the bar and separate restaurant.

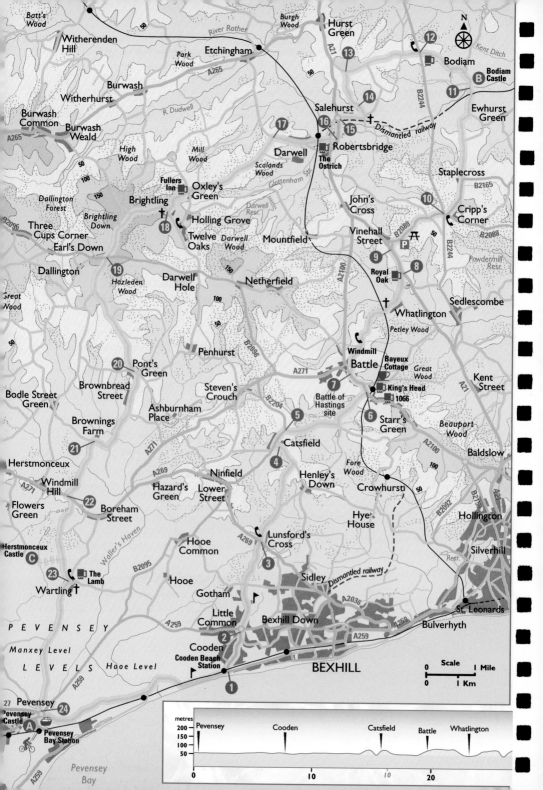

Route description

Leave Pevensey Bay Station. TL onto the A259 then take RHF onto the minor road towards Bexhill.

1 Pass Cooden Beach Station and TL.
7km (4.5 miles)

2 Arrive Little Common roundabout, SO.

3 Arrive at XR with A269, SO. Keep left at the next two junctions. *12km (7.5 miles)*

4 Ride through Catsfield to TJ with B2204, TR.

5 TR following SP Battle. *16km (10 miles)*

6 Arrive TJ with A2100, TL into Battle.

7 TR following SP Whatlington. Note the windmill on your left. *20km (12.5 miles)*

8 TL onto A21, PH on the left.

9 TR onto B2089, with picnic area and forest walk signed to your right.
24.5km (15 miles)

10 Cross B2244 and onto B2165. SO on when the B road bears right.

11 Pass entrance to Bodiam Castle on your right, bear left and through Bodiam village to continue the ride. *30km (18.5 miles)*

12 Arrive XR with B2244, SO.

13 TL (easy to miss!) down single track road to Salehurst. *35.5km (22 miles)*

14 Through Salehurst and arrive at the TJ by the church, TR.

15 Junction with A21, TL into Robertsbridge.

16 TR, passing the station and the Ostrich PH.

17 TL following SP to Brightling.
40km (25 miles)

18 Arrive at Brightling TJ, TR and bear left when the road forks, following the edge of a wood. *45.5km (28.5 miles)*

19 Arrive at XR with B2096, SO.

20 Through Pont's Street, then TR to Brownbread Street. *52km (32.5 miles)*

21 TL at Brownings Farm.
55.5km (34.5 miles)

22 Arrive at TJ with A271, TL then first right SP to Wartling, passing Herstmonceux Castle.

23 Arrive Wartling, TR following SP to Pevensey. *59.5km (37 miles)*

24 Arrive at TJ with A259 in Pevensey, TR to finish ride at Pevensey Bay Station.
65km (40.5 miles)

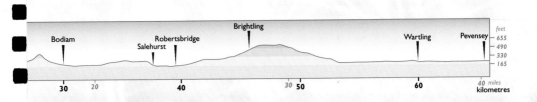

TOP OF THE DOWNS TO THE FOREST RIDGE

Route information

Distance 68.5km (42.5 miles)

Grade Strenuous

Terrain Suitable for adults and older teenagers, using hybrid or all-terrain bikes. The ride opens with a challenging climb over the top of the South Downs, then up the Cuckmere Valley and into the rolling lanes of the Weald, finishing with a stiff climb onto the South Downs Way and 6.5 km (4 miles) off-road cycling.

Time to allow Up to 5 hours.

Getting there by car Seaford is on the A259 Brighton to Eastbourne road, with pay parking in the town.

Getting there by train Seaford Station is served by Connex South Central from Brighton and Eastbourne. Bicycles are carried free during off-peak times, and timetable information is available on (0345) 484950.

From Seaford on the South Coast through Sussex villages and past Arlington and Barcombe Reservoirs, returning to Seaford through Glynde and Alfriston. This is one of the few rides that means climbing to the top of the South Downs – twice – before dropping into the Cuckmere River Valley and running north towards the remains of the Weald forests. The climb is known as High and Over (it is high, and you'll be glad when it's over). The Weald forests were extensively felled to feed the furnaces of the Sussex iron industry and the trees were further damaged by nature in the great storm of 1987. This area of Sussex is the Forest Ridge, formed when the sandstone hills of the Weald were eroded into the area's characteristic hills and valleys. The ride passes Piltdown, once an anonymous Sussex village, where Piltdown Man was found – an attempt to fake the fossil remains of an early human. The ride passes through Alfriston twice, so you have plenty of opportunities to make the most of this most beautiful Downs village.

Places of interest along the route

Ⓐ Alfriston Clergy House, Alfriston

In 1896 Alfriston Clergy House was the first property to be bought by the National Trust. It is a thatched 14th-century Wealden Hall House and the medieval hall and several rooms are open to the public. The house has a charming cottage garden, containing many rare plants, that affords views of the Cuckmere River. The house is open daily from March to October 1030-1700, or dusk if earlier. Charge. Telephone (01323) 870001.

Ⓑ Bentley Wildfowl and Motor Museum, Halland, near Lewes

The Bentley Wildfowl and Motor Museum offers plenty of interest for car fans and naturalists. The estate is home to over 115 species of wildfowl and a motor museum of vintage and veteran cars. There are also gardens, a picnic area and a children's adventure playground. Open daily from March to October, from 1030 with last admissions at 1630 (1700 in July and August) and during the winter open at weekends only, from 1030 with last admissions at 1600. Charge. Telephone (01825) 840573.

Ⓒ Glynde Place,
Glynde, Lewes

Glynde Place, a magnificent Elizabethan manor built in 1569, has been home to the same family for over 800 years. It boasts elegant architecture, fine art and antiques, an exhibition on the English Civil War and a glimpse into the lives of the former inhabitants. The park adjoining the house was landscaped over a century ago and has deliberately been managed to encourage wildflowers and wildlife. A flower festival is held here in September. Tearoom. Charge. Open Easter Day and Easter Monday, Sundays and Bank Holidays during May; and Wednesday, Thursday and Sunday from June to September 1400-1700. Telephone (01273) 858224.

Ⓓ Middle Farm,
near Firle, Lewes

The Countryside Centre at Middle Farm contains a comprehensive farm shop, garden section, cider centre, tourist information centre and traditional butchery, all set within a 1483 hectare (600 acre) working farm. Tearoom offering substantial snacks and baking in either the picturesque courtyard or inside by an open fire. Free admission. Open daily, all year round 1000-1700. Telephone (01323) 490222.

Drusillas Park is also on the ride – see Route 3 for information.

Food and drink

Refreshments are available at Alfriston Clergy House, Bentley Estate, Glynde Place and Middle Farm. Alfriston is a popular tourist spot, and there are too many quaint cafés to list.

Ⓓ Star Inn, Alfriston

Low-beamed ceilings, real ale and a very old world atmosphere. A distinctive red lion carving stands outside this pub.

Ⓓ Cricketers Arms, Berwick

A quiet, quaint pub built in a row of cottages, with beer from Harvey's brewery in nearby Lewes. Open fires, stone-flagged floor, and excellent atmosphere for lunchtime and evening meals.

Ⓓ Laughing Fish, Isfield

A CAMRA-recommended pub, with the added quirky interest of having the beer cellar naturally refrigerated by an underground stream. Serves local Harvey's beer, and bar meals both at lunchtimes and in the evenings.

Route description

Leave Seaford Station onto the A259 and TR following SP Eastbourne.

1 SP Alfriston, TL, following the road as it bears right. Steep climb ahead.

2 Arrive Alfriston, SO through the village.
5.5km (3.5 miles)

3 Arrive at roundabout at A27 and go SO.
7.5km (5 miles)

4 After passing Arlington Reservoir, TL along a road that bears left then right.
10km (6 miles)

5 Road bears left, TR here.

6 SP Laughton, TL.   *16km (10 miles)*

7 Arrive at XR with the B2124 at Laughton, SO.

8 Arrive at TJ with the B2192, TL.
19.5km (12 miles)

9 TR towards Bentley Wildfowl and Motor Museum, passing the entrance.

10 Road bends right, then SP Isfield, TL.
25.5km (16 miles)

11 Arrive at XR with A26, and SO.

12 TR into Isfield, through the village and continue north.   *28km (17.5 miles)*

13 Take LHF in the road, leading SO.
32km (20 miles)

14 After passing through Shortbridge, bear left to continue the route.   *33km (20.5 miles)*

15 TL, after passing golf course on your right hand side and before you reach the A272. Continue over River Ouse, Longford Stream and Bevern Stream.

16 Arrive Barcombe Cross and TL, riding carefully on this narrow road back over the River Ouse.   *41km (25.5 miles)*

17 Arrive at TJ with A26 and TR.

18 TL off A26 towards Ringmer. TR onto B2192 in Ringmer.   *45km (28 miles)*

19 Just out of Ringmer, TL to Glynde, through Glynde and across the railway crossing at Glynde Station. Keep left towards the A27.

20 Arrive at TJ with the A27 and TL, then turn first right SP West Firle, through West Firle following the road straight up the South Downs. To visit Middle Farm, continue along A27. Middle Farm is signed to your left after 2km (1 mile).

21 Meet South Downs Way, TL towards Alfriston, ready for 6.5km (4 miles) of rough riding. Superb views along this section, past Firle Beacon.   *56.5km (35 miles)*

22 Arrive Alfriston, TR following SP Seaford.   *63km (39 miles)*

23 Arrive Seaford, join A259 and TR to finish ride at Seaford Station.
68.5km (42.5 miles)

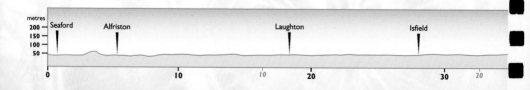

THE SOUTH DOWNS WAY – PETERSFIELD TO BIGNOR

Route information

 Distance 69km (43 miles)

 Grade Strenuous

Terrain Half of the ride is on good roads, half on the South Downs Way, an off-road track with a varied surface including bumpy dirt tracks covered in gravel, small rocks and tree roots, suitable for mountain bikes and only the most robust hybrid bicycles. There are some demanding climbs and fast descents on loose surfaces, and you should ride with care.

Time to allow 5-6 hours.

Getting there by car Petersfield is on the A3 London to Portsmouth road. Turn onto the A272 which has signs to the station for pay and display car parking. There is also parking at Heath Pond, an excellent point to start the ride. However, you can avoid the stiff climb out of South Harting by starting the ride at Tower Hill car park.

Getting there by train Petersfield is on South West Trains London Waterloo to Portsmouth line. Telephone (0345) 484950 for information.

From Petersfield using the South Downs Way to Sutton, and returning to Petersfield along lanes at the foot of the Downs. This is a strenuous ride that takes you across a substantial part of the South Downs Way, allows you to see the superb mosaics and remains at the Bignor Roman Villa, then provides a selection of tree-lined, quiet, rolling lanes to return you to Petersfield. The return lanes run along the foot of the Downs that you have just ridden along the top of, so look to your left occasionally and marvel at the climbs and descents you've just done. The South Downs Way follows the course of an ancient ridgeway, and a map of its complete length will show you that it is littered with burial mounds, forts and protective earthworks from Bronze and Iron age settlements.

Places of interest along the route

Ⓐ South Harting

A pretty village, reputedly the most westerly in Sussex. It was home to the writer Anthony Trollope, author of the *Barchester Chronicles*.

Ⓑ Bignor Roman Villa, Bignor, near Pulborough

A magnificent display of mosaic floors and Roman artefacts contained in a museum that tells the story of the roman villa. Gift shop and cafeteria. Open March, April, May and October (closed Mondays except Bank Holidays) 1000-1700; daily from June to September 1000-1800. Charge. Telephone (01798) 869259.

Food and drink

Petersfield town centre has a good range of shops — stock up before the ride! Refreshments are available in South Harting and at the Bignor Roman Villa.

The Ship, South Harting
A CAMRA-recommended pub, with low beams and a substantial menu.

White Hart, South Harting
Opposite the Ship with a garden and bar meals at lunchtimes and in the evenings.

White House, Sutton
This pub is conveniently situated on the route after 35.5km (22 miles).

The Cricketers, Graffham
A quiet local country pub with open fires, a beamed ceiling, locally-brewed real ale and a substantial restaurant and bar meal menu.

Bluebell Inn, Cocking
Accessible from the off-road section of the ride (it is signed on the South Downs Way), and you ride right past it on the way back.

Cocking Post Office and Stores
Shop open Monday-Friday 0600-1800, Saturday 0630-1800, Sunday 0700-1600.

Route description

Leave Petersfield Station, XR, TR. Then XR SO, road bears left. Into Hylton Road, XR, SP South Harting SO.

1 Pass car park at Heath Pond. Car drivers can start the ride here. Follow SP to South Harting.

2 Arrive South Harting village. At SP Emsworth, Chichester, TR. **6.5km (4 miles)**

3 SP Chichester B2141, TL.

4 Pass the road turning, a stile, then you should see a track to your left with a finger post signing the South Downs Way (SDW).
8km (5 miles)

5 Follow the SDW and note it bears to the right, around the south side of Beacon Hill.

6 Easy to miss TL as you descend the hill — look for the SDW fingerpost.
10.5km (6.5 miles)

7 Arrive Buriton Farm, follow SDW signs first right then TL.

8 After a steep climb, reach the top of Linch Down. **16km (10 miles)**

9 Reach A286, straight across.

10 Look for the small obelisk on your right outside the English Timber buildings — there is a drinking water tap here, the last before Amberley, so fill up! Continue up onto woodland ridge. **26.5km (16.5 miles)**

11 Fast, steep descent off Littleton Down — caution, there is a sharp right hand bend at the bottom of the descent.

12 Cross A285. **28km (17.5 miles)**

13 The SDW enters the National Trust Slindon Estate, running along the right-hand edge of a field. Exit field, SP SDW TL.

14 SDW arrives at Bignor Hill car park. Follow SP Bignor and Londinium pointing down a tarmac road to the left of SDW. A steep descent follows. **32km (20 miles)**

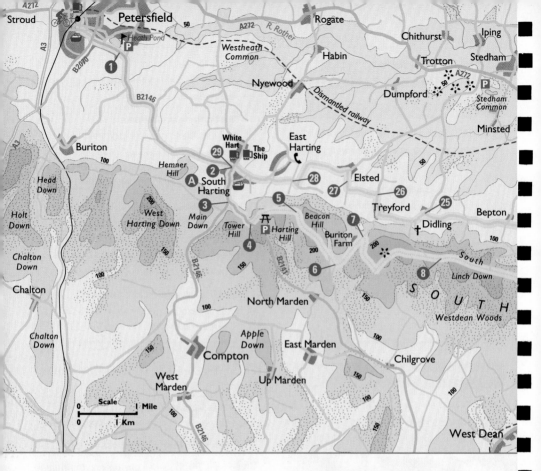

15 Through farm. On exiting the farm TR follow SP to visit Bignor Roman Villa, or TL through Bignor village towards Sutton.

16 Follow signs for Sutton and Duncton. Arrive Sutton, road bears right.

35km (21.5 miles)

17 XR, SP Duncton, TL.

18 Meet A285, SP Duncton, TL then SP Graffham 3 miles, TR.

19 XR SP Graffham TL. **41.5km (26 miles)**

20 In the centre of Graffham, arrive at a junction without a sign TR.

21 Road bends left, then sharp right. Follow SP Cocking. **45.5km (28.5 miles)**

22 XR TL heading to Hoyle.

23 Arrive at XR with track ahead. SO onto the track, heading for Cocking.

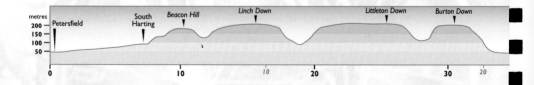

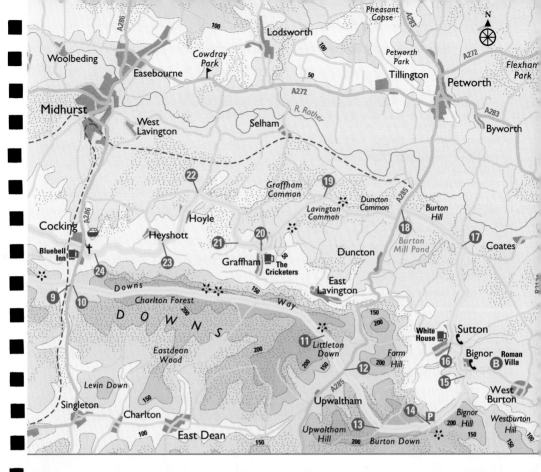

24 Into Cocking, passing a war memorial and striking church on your right. You emerge by Cocking Post Office and Stores and the Bluebell Inn. TL past the Post Office onto the A286, and then immediate right into Bell Lane. Continue along this narrow road.

51km (31.5 miles)

25 At Didling SP Treyford TL.

26 SP Elsted and Harting TL.

57km (35 miles)

27 Enter Elsted. At the staggered XR SP Harting and Petersfield TL.

28 XR SP Petersfield and South Harting, SO to South Harting. *60.5km (37.5 miles)*

29 In South Harting SP Petersfield B2146 TR. Follow the road to Petersfield – to Heath Pond if you left your car there or on to the station. *69km (43 miles)*

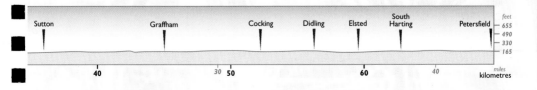

BOGNOR REGIS, SELSEY BILL AND CHICHESTER HARBOUR

Route information

Distance 93km (58 miles)

Grade Moderate

Terrain This is a rare Sussex ride – much of it is flat! The middle part of the ride runs to the north of Chichester, where the dip slope of the South Downs has carved the landscape into hills and valleys – the ride just takes in the lower slopes of these, so that the terrain is undulating rather than the challengingly hilly countryside characteristic of Sussex and the Downs. Suitable for all road and all-terrain bikes (ATBs), although ATBs should have high-pressure road tyres fitted.

Time to allow 5-7 hours, including stops.

Getting there by car Bognor Regis is on the A259 Chichester to Littlehampton road. Car parking on the sea front, less than 1km (0.5 miles) from the station.

Getting there by train Connex South Central serves Bognor Regis from Bournemouth, Portsmouth Harbour and Brighton. For timetable enquiries telephone (0345) 484950.

A loop from Bognor Regis to Selsey Bill and through the inland villages around Chichester, returning to Bognor Regis. This ride offers the adventurous cyclist the chance to take to the water on a boat trip around Chichester harbour from Itchenor. The flat terrain makes for easy cycling – unless there is a blustery south-westerly blowing off the Channel. This area is heaving with ancient British history. The 450,000-year-old fossil remains of the earliest known British hominid were discovered at Boxgrove; Chichester was the Roman town of Noviomagus; and Fishbourne to the west of Chichester is the site of the largest Roman palace yet discovered.

Places of interest along the route

Ⓐ Pagham Harbour

Pagham has not actually been a harbour for about 500 years, owing to silting. However, you may be rewarded by packing a pair of binoculars since these mud flats attract birds in huge numbers. More than 200 species have been recorded, and marine mammals – seals and porpoises – have been seen in the bay.

Ⓑ Chichester Harbour

The harbour (an Area of Outstanding Natural Beauty) is a further wildlife haven –- thousands of acres of water, mud flats, beaches and sand dunes support a varied population of birds, while the sheltered waters are often equally teeming with boating humans. You can join them with a boat tour around the harbour, starting from West Itchenor. The ferry between

West Itchenor and Bosham operates from April to September at weekends and daily during the school holidays. Telephone Chichester Tourist Information Centre on (01243) 775888 for further details on the ferry and the harbour tours.

ⓒ Bosham

A National Trust site, and rightly so with its sea front cottages, church and village green. Bosham contributed the name to Lord Bosham, the Earl of Emsworth's aristocratic but dim-witted son in PG Wodehouse's famous series of books about Blandings Castle.

ⓓ Uppark House,
Uppark, South Harting

This National Trust property was destroyed by fire in 1989 and has been completely renovated to the fine condition it was in on the day before the fire. The gardens have been restored to their Capability Brown style and there are woodland walks. Restaurant and shop. Open from the end of March to the end of October, Sunday-Thursday. Walks open 1000-1730, garden open 1200-1730 and house open 1300-1700. Charge. This is a much visited property and booking is advisable. Telephone (01730) 825857 for a recorded message giving further information.

ⓔ Tangmere Museum of Military Aviation, Tangmere Airfield, near Chichester

Tangmere was a front line airfield during the Battle of Britain. Many of the aerial battles were fought over Sussex as the RAF tried to stop the German Luftwaffe bombing London. Tangmere Museum chronicles this struggle as part of the history of military flying, and the museum contains replica Hurricane and Spitfire fighters of Battle of Britain vintage, along with later fighter aircraft used by the RAF. Open daily from March to October 1000-1730; and in November and February 1000-1630. Charge. Telephone (01243) 775223.

The Vandelian Folly in the grounds at Uppark

Route description

Leave Bognor Regis Station, TL, SO the XR towards the seafront. Join the B2166 and follow this road inland towards Chichester.

1 Arrive XR on outskirts of Bognor, SO.

2 Arrive TJ, TL onto B2145.
8.5km (5 miles)

3 After passing through Sidlesham, TR. The road forks, take LHF.

4 Arrive at a TJ, TL towards East Wittering.
18km (11 miles)

5 Arrive at TJ with B2198, TL then TR onto B2179. Follow this road through East and West Wittering.

6 Arrive XR TL following SP West Itchenor.
27.5km (17 miles)

7 Arrive West Itchenor to catch the ferry across the channel to Bosham.

8 Leave the ferry, TR to Bosham Hoe, then follow the road left to Bosham.
30km (18.5 miles)

9 Arrive Bosham. Keep left, then right through the village. *35km (21.5 miles)*

10 Arrive roundabout with A259, SO onto B2146.

11 B2146 bears right, TL over stream then arrive at TJ and TL. *38km (23.5 miles)*

12 Arrive TJ with B2147 and TR.

13 TL just before the chapel on the left of the road. Follow the road through Aldsworth.
44.5km (27.5 miles)

14 Take RHF and proceed through Stansted Forest. *46.5km (29 miles)*

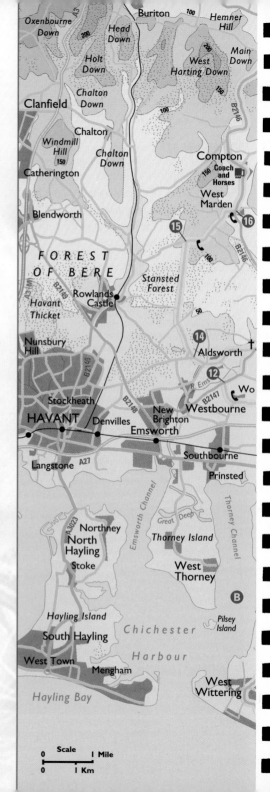

15 Arrive TJ, TR following SP West Marden.
51km (31.5 miles)

16 Arrive West Marden XR, TL. Follow B2146 through Compton and to Uppark House.

17 TR onto B2141 SP Chichester and go through Chilgrove, bearing right opposite the church. *59km (36.5 miles)*

18 TR at A286, follow SP Chichester, through Mid Lavant. *70km (43.5 miles)*

19 TL following SP East Lavant.

20 Arrive XR, SO then TL at next XR.

21 TR at Hotel Waterbeach.
76km (47 miles)

22 Arrive at XR with A285, SO through Boxgrove.

23 Arrive at XR with A27 – cross with care. TR then TL through Tangmere.
79.5km 49.5 miles)

24 TL onto B2144.

25 Arrive at TJ with A259. TL then TR.
84.5km (52.5 miles)

26 Arrive XR, TL along B2166 into Bognor Regis. Bear left with B2166 just before the pier. SO at XR, continue to next major XR, SO to the station on your right. *93km (58 miles)*

Food and drink

📖 **The Lamb, Steyne Street, Bognor Regis**
Lunches and evening meals except Sunday and Monday evenings, along with a selection of local real ale, which can be drunk in front of open fires, or in the beer garden.

📖 **Crab and Lobster, Sidlesham**
Open fires, CAMRA-commended beers and an attractive garden.

📖 **Lamb Inn, West Wittering**
A short diversion off the route along the B2178 between directions 4 and 5. A quiet pub with a good range of beer and a large menu, served lunchtimes and evenings, except Sunday evenings in winter.

📖 **Coach and Horses, Compton**
Serves Fuller's and a range of four guest real ales. Meals available lunchtimes and evenings.

📖 **Earl of March, Lavant**
Good value food at lunchtimes and in the evenings. The garden gives splendid views of the South Downs.

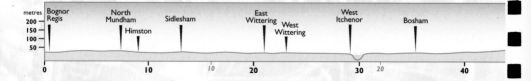

Uppark House

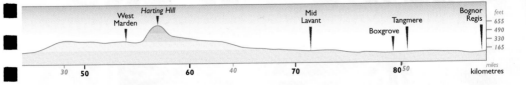

THE SOUTH DOWNS WAY
AND THE DOWNS LINK

Route information

Distance 112.5 km (70 miles)

Grade Strenuous

Terrain The first part of the ride is on the hilly South Downs Way (SDW), with some steep climbs and demanding, technical off-road riding. From Bramber to Guildford, the Downs Link (DL) is a former railway track, largely flat or with very gentle inclines. The surface of both tracks is covered with loose gravel and can be bumpy and rutted. This ride is suitable only for all-terrain bikes.

Time to allow 8-12 hours riding time – the ride could be done over two days.

Getting there by car Eastbourne is on the A22 and A259 and is is a busy seaside resort with limited parking. Overnight parking is available at the National Car Park's multi-storey car park in Trinity Place (just off the seafront between the bandstand and Carpet Gardens). Telephone (01323) 734812 for information. It you do leave a car at Eastbourne, finish the ride at Guildford Station for train services back to Eastbourne.

Getting there by train Eastbourne Station is on the Brighton to Ashford line, served by Connex South Central. Trains run from London Charing Cross to Brighton, change at Brighton for Eastbourne. Bicycles are carried free off-peak. Telephone (0345) 484950 for information.

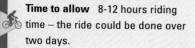

From Eastbourne on the Sussex Coast, along the SDW to Bramber and north along the DL to Guildford. This ride takes you along the spine of ancient Sussex on the SDW, which was a ridgeway track for centuries before it was opened in 1972 as a long-distance path for walkers, horse riders and cyclists. Although there are some excellent, fast descents, ride with care because of the loose surface and always give way to pedestrians. The SDW has remains of its ancient past along its length, with Iron Age forts, defensive earthworks and tumuli (burial mounds) visible beside the trail.

The DL is a relic of Sussex's industrial past – the track bed of the former Shoreham to Itchingfield Junction line and the Horsham to Guildford Railway, closed during the 1960s. The redundant track was developed into the DL by three local authorities. Disused stations, cuttings and bridges show the track's railway heritage, and the DL is the flattest (and easiest) route through the Weald between Sussex and Surrey. You might like to do this ride over two days. Truleight Hill Youth Hostel (01903) 813419 is approximately halfway along the ride. Telephone the Youth Hostel Association on

0171 836 1036 for information. The booklet Along the South Downs Way, *available from Tourist Information Centres, lists overnight stops close to the route.*

Places of interest along the route

A Long Man of Wilmington, on the SDW, east of Alfriston

The Long Man is a giant figure cut into the hillside alongside the path of the SDW. There are several theories as to the figure's origin: fertility symbol or perhaps an ancient warrior. Lack of historical evidence leaves this open to interpretation. The site of the Long Man is owned by the Sussex Archaeological Society, telephone (01273) 486260.

B Alfriston

The village is quite beautiful and is well worth a visit to see the close-packed thatched cottages in their traditional village setting. Alfriston Clergy House, a thatched 14th-century Wealden Hall House (see Route 3 for details) is situated in the village and there are plenty of tea shops to help slake a cyclist's thirst. Telephone the Boship Tourist Information Centre on (01323) 442667 for further information.

C Ditchling Beacon, Ditchling

One of the highest points of the South Downs at 248m (813 feet). The beacon is crowned by the traces of an Iron Age fort and surrounded by nature reserves, with extensive views over the Downs.

D Jack and Jill Windmills, Clayton, near Hassocks

Jill, a post mill, was built in 1821 in Brighton and moved to her present site in 1852. The mill was restored to working order before suffering much damage in the great storm of 1987, but is now milling again. Jack, a tower mill, was built in 1866 and is privately owned. Jill is open from May to September, most Sundays and Bank Holidays 1200-1600. Admission free but donations welcome. Telephone (01273) 843263 in the evenings for information.

E Devil's Dyke, near Poynings

The Devil's Dyke is a natural valley. Legend has it that the Devil tried to cut a valley into the Downs, hoping to flood the area and its churches. He was foiled by St Cuthman and a local woman who faked a false dawn with candles, forcing the Devil to flee. There is a direction indicator opposite the Dyke Hotel showing the prominent points in the view from the summit.

F Bramber Castle, Bramber

Built in Norman times, probably to replace an earlier Saxon fort, Bramber's castle was destroyed by Parliamentary forces during the Civil War. A gaunt 'tooth', 23m (76 feet) high, is all that remains of the keep, but you can still see how it guarded the river which once lapped at the foot of its mound. It is now in the care of English Heritage and is open (free of charge) at all reasonable times. Telephone (01732) 778000.

G Baynards Station, Rudgwick

The station was privately built by a local landowner when the Horsham Railway was laid. When Dr Beeching closed the line in the 1960s the station was turned into a private house. It is a beautiful sight from the route, especially in spring and summer, when the former station is a mass of flowers. The film *The Railway Children* was partly filmed here.

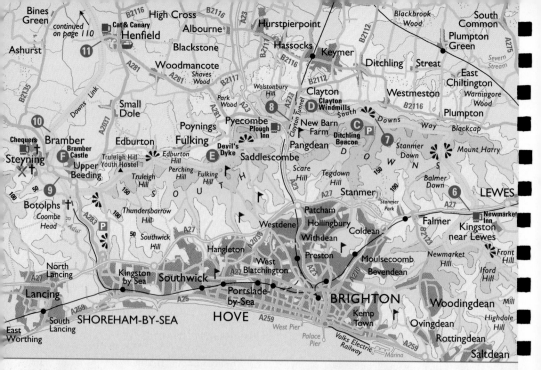

continued on page 110

Route description

Leave Eastbourne Station, TL and head towards the seafront (B2103) and TR, following the road out of the town to the west. TR onto a bridleway that joins SDW at Warren Hill. TL onto the SDW.

1 Cross A259.

2 Arrive Jevington, at the road TR briefly (along road) then left past church rejoining SDW track. After a time you will pass the Long Man of Wilmington on your right.

10.5km (6.5 miles)

3 Arrive Alfriston. The SDW joins a road, SO across bridge then TL into Alfriston. To rejoin the SDW, bear right opposite the church, along a residential road, then onto the chalky track, climbing to Bostall Hill. Descend past the car park then climb to Firle Beacon. Pass the radio masts at Beddingham Hill. Track bears left, then begins a rapid descent through Itford Farm to meet the A26. Cross A26 onto narrow lane, follow SP to Southease. Cross the railway at the crossing.

4 Enter Southease. TR towards Rodmell.

26.5km (16.5 miles)

5 Enter Rodmell and TL opposite the Abergavenny Arms pub, climb out of Rodmell along a road, then the SDW turns right, for a steep climb past Mill Hill and over Front Hill and Iford Hill. Join a concreted farm road, and when it bends left, go through a gate and

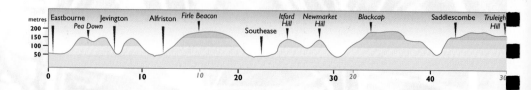

follow the track along the top of the hill until it bears left, then right towards the A27.

6 Arrive A27 and cross with care (36km/22.5 miles). TR for a short distance then TL onto the SDW, following SDW fingerposts through a patch of woodland before climbing to Balmer Down. After passing under electricity lines, the SDW continues to the left towards Ditchling Beacon.

right and continue due west on the flint track, climbing to Fulking Hill, Perching Hill and Edburton Hill before bearing left to pass Truleigh Hill Youth Hostel. After the hostel, SO until the you reach the A283. TL along A283 then after 170m (186 yards), TR into the layby, through the gate, meet the DL and TR.

62km (38.5 miles)

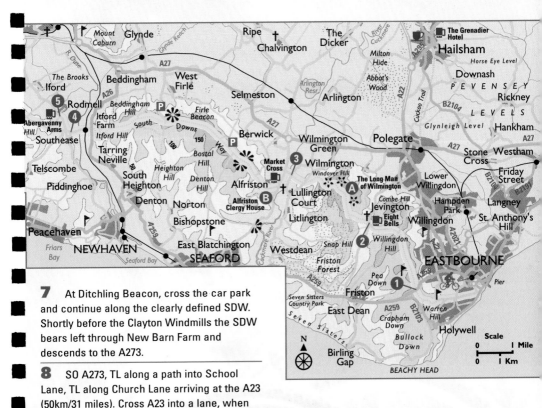

7 At Ditchling Beacon, cross the car park and continue along the clearly defined SDW. Shortly before the Clayton Windmills the SDW bears left through New Barn Farm and descends to the A273.

8 SO A273, TL along a path into School Lane, TL along Church Lane arriving at the A23 (50km/31 miles). Cross A23 into a lane, when the lane bears left go SO onto SDW. Continue to Saddlescombe, SO across road and climb to Summer Down. Pass the Devil's Dyke on your

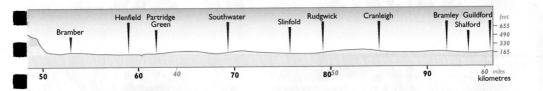

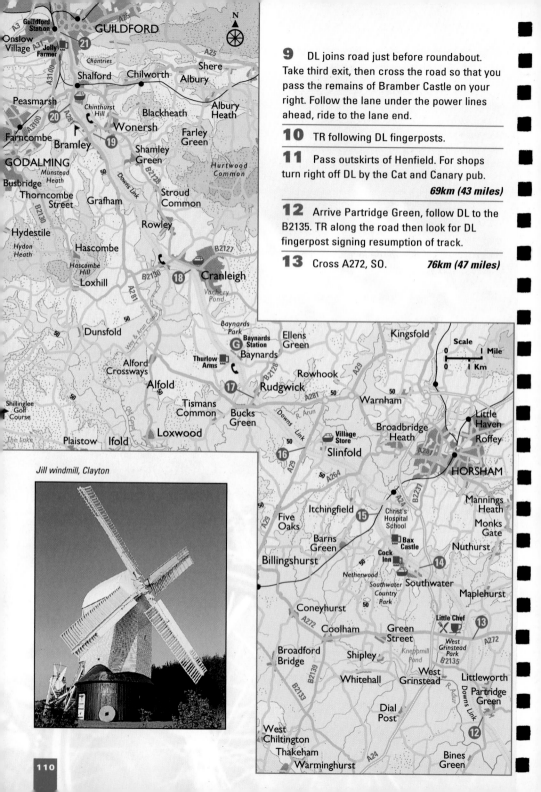

9 DL joins road just before roundabout. Take third exit, then cross the road so that you pass the remains of Bramber Castle on your right. Follow the lane under the power lines ahead, ride to the lane end.

10 TR following DL fingerposts.

11 Pass outskirts of Henfield. For shops turn right off DL by the Cat and Canary pub.

69km (43 miles)

12 Arrive Partridge Green, follow DL to the B2135. TR along the road then look for DL fingerpost signing resumption of track.

13 Cross A272, SO. *76km (47 miles)*

Jill windmill, Clayton

14 Arrive Southwater and leave the trackbed where indicated, into Andrews Lane. SO at the XR.

15 Arrive Christ's Hospital school, pass the school on your right, then join the lane and TL across the bridge to the TJ. TR then rejoin the DL trackbed at the bridge ahead.

83.5km (52 miles)

16 Cross A29.

17 Arrive Rudgwick. Between Rudgwick and Baynards Station, the bridleway is signed off the main track. Follow the bridleway signs that will take you left off the footpath. Up a slope the bridleway bears right down the hill to meet a road. TR along road, over the bridge, then the DL starts again on the right, passing under the bridge you have just crossed.

18 Pass Cranleigh. *98km (61 miles)*

19 Arrive at road, SO through the remains of Bramley and Wonersh Station. At the next bridge, ignore DL signs and go SO under bridge.

20 Track ends abruptly, rising to join the A281. TR following A281 into Guildford.

21 Pass the Jolly Farmer pub then Debenhams on your left, arrive at traffic-light controlled roundabout, take third exit, following signs to Guildford Station.

112.5km (70 miles)

Food and drink

Eight Bells, High Street, Jevington
A quiet pub with a beer garden, lunchtime and evening food.

Market Cross,
Waterloo Square, Alfriston
Another supposedly haunted pub, although the ghosts detract neither from the atmosphere, nor the lunches and evening meals.

Chequers, Bramber High Street, Bramber
A CAMRA-recommended pub which serves substantial lunchtime and evening food.

Little Chef, where the DL crosses the A272 at direction 13
Turn right for burgers and chips nourishment.

Bax Castle,
Two Mile Ash Road, between
Southwater and Christ's Hospital
Situated to the right of the DL, this quiet pub serves lunchtime and evening meals. Attractive garden.

Thurlow Arms,
Baynards Station, Rudgwick
Bar meals, beer garden and real ale.

Slinfold has a well-stocked village store, reached by turning off the route after the obvious caravan site on your right just after Slinfold. Signs will take you to Slinfold High Street. There are shops in Cranleigh, Shalford, Henfield and Cocking.

THE CYCLISTS' TOURING CLUB

The CTC is Britain's largest national cycling organisation. Founded in 1878, the CTC has over 40,000 members throughout the UK and overseas, around 200 local groups and 200 independent affiliated clubs. The CTC provides essential services for all leisure cyclists, whether you ride on- or off-road, and works to promote cycling and protect cyclists' interests.

CTC membership makes day-to-day cycling easier. An expert cycling engineer will answer your technical queries about cycle buying, maintenance and equipment. If you get ambitious about your cycling, the CTC's Touring Department has reams of information about cycling anywhere from Avon to Zimbabwe. The shop sells a wide variety of clothing, accessories, books, maps and guide books. The handbook lists practically everything a cyclist could wish to know.

Cycling is one of the healthiest activities there is – it raises your metabolism, burns fat and tones muscle. However, accidents do happen, and the CTC's services mean that when you ride, you are protected by free third party liability of up to £1 million, and by our legal assistance to pursue civil claims.

Club members also receive *Cycle Touring and Campaigning* magazine free six times a year. CT&C regards independent journalism as a service to CTC members. With reports on cycle trips all over the globe, forensic tests on bikes and equipment, and the most vigorous and effective pro-bike campaigning stance anywhere, CT&C is required reading for any cyclist.

The CTC works on behalf of all Britain's 20 million cycle owners. It is lobbying for lower speed limits on country lanes; campaigning so that you can carry bikes on trains; working with local authorities to make towns more cycle-friendly, to ensure that roads are designed to meet cyclists' needs and kept well maintained; making sure that bridleways are kept open; and negotiating cyclists' access to canal towpaths.

Don't be put off by the word 'touring' in the title. Mountain bikers, Sunday potterers, bicycle commuters, families on a day out – cycling is easier and safer with the CTC's knowledge and services in your saddlebag. You will be protecting and informing yourself, and strengthening the campaign for cyclists' rights, on- and off-road.

For further information contact:
Cyclists' Touring Club
Cotterell House
69 Meadrow
Godalming
Surrey
GU7 3HS

Telephone (01483) 417217
Fax (01483) 426994
e-mail: cycling@ctc.org.uk
Web page: http://www.ctc.org.uk